You Can Live On Half Your Income

Camilla Dayton Luckey

Zondervan Publishing House
of The Zondervan Corporation
Grand Rapids, Michigan

YOU CAN LIVE ON HALF YOUR INCOME
© 1982 by Camilla Dayton Luckey

Library of Congress Cataloging in Publication Data

Luckey, Camilla Dayton.
    You can live on half your income.

    Includes index.
    1. Consumer education. I. Title.
TX335.L78 1982   640   82-16081
ISBN 0-310-45581-2

Edited by Judith E. Markham
Designed by Louise Bauer

Printed in the United States of America

83 84 85 86 87 88 / 9 8 7 6 5 4 3 2 1

To
my
mother

Contents

Introduction

This book is for two types of people: those who think they could live on half their income and those who think they could not. The dividing line is not drawn in dollars. Neither is it characterized by necessity; the way the economy tilts, we may all soon find ourselves in "reduced circumstances."

A small number of brave souls determine to scrape by indefinitely on what the rest of us consider starvation budgets. Some make political statements by living in poverty; they decry the financial injustices of the world. Others feel overwhelmed by our accelerating society; they try to turn back the clock to the simpler, slower days of our grandparents, when a dollar stashed under the mattress was worth as much the day it was pulled out as the day it was put there several years earlier. A rare few realize that money has little to do with what they want from life; they prefer to focus precious time and energy on what they know satisfies. And then there are those who accept a divinely given mandate; their voluntary simplicity expresses both social and spiritual values.

But the majority of people are like my friends.

Since I began telling them about this book, I've learned just how far eyebrows can rise. Virtually every comment was a duplicate or a variation of the following four which, collectively, describe the line between those who think they could and those who think they could not live on half their income.

"What do I do with the other half?" The rarest response—but valid—this one floored me the first time I heard it. *What* other half? This is not a "live on half; invest the rest" how-to. Neither is it a morose lament for lost income and, ergo, lost pleasures. It's a pep talk. Low income needn't mean low spirits.

"How soon can I get a copy?" was the most common response. Graduate school, self-employment, a less remunerative but more satisfying job, children, retirement: maybe these dreams, deflated by our inflationary economy, *are* possible! For these people, money is not the object in life. But the hardship they perceived to be necessary while they put life to their dreams has kept their dreams just that. And since they couldn't have their dreams, they settled for cash. But spiraling inflation is robbing them of that too, and they're ready to take a second look. If this book can help them see how to balance the scales—work and money on the one side and the rest of their lives on the other—they might try.

"I admit I could live on half my income, but not in the style to which I am or would like to be accustomed." True, perhaps. But they might live longer. Literally every friend who gave this response has ulcers or high blood pressure or both. No matter how much money they have, it's not enough. Despite abundant financial resources, the determination to follow their dreams is an almost impossible detour. These friends are unwilling, unable, to lay down their dollars for their dreams. What they want from this book is the stuff of bestsellers—a how-to capitalizing on greed: *How To Take Advantage of the Hard Times Around You; How To Make Someone Else Make Your Money Grow Without You Really Working.* This book won't do that, but it will help them get every penny's worth of every dollar they already have. It may even change a few attitudes.

"You're not going to tell folks you *prayed* your way through this year, are you?" was the fourth type of response. My answer? Yes, I am and I did—although I didn't want to. It's humbling to admit I couldn't do it by myself. Through prayer comes strength (I need it every time I find myself in a store with credit easily available). But it's up to me to exercise that strength, to practice self-restraint, to keep my priorities foremost, to use my own noggin and make wise application of my resources. Greed and the desire for instant gratification I must constantly, consciously quash. I know I can't do it alone.

1

Bench Marks

*Hope deferred makes the heart sick,
but a longing fulfilled is a tree of life.*

PROVERBS 13:12

Two years ago I became a Christian. At that time there was a lot of weeding to be done in the garden that is my life. Strangely enough, in the weeding process I discovered the root common to all the weeds: greed. Usually it was greed for money, but in all cases it was for what I considered to be my own best interests. This shouldn't have seemed so strange. The love of money, the apostle Paul once said (usually quoted without acknowledgment), is the root of all evil. For my money he couldn't have chosen a more apt metaphor. This root is so insidious that its offspring are like crabgrass. They sprout anywhere, thrive everywhere. Their subsurface network is indestructible unless you rip up the whole property, weed out every last bit. A tedious job and messy, but that's what I began to do, with the help of the master gardener.

About the time of my conversion (within a matter of weeks, actually, but that's another *long* story), I conceived what was to be our second child. Obviously it was time for changes, some of them financial. How would we manage a second child and all the concomitant expense without finding more financial resources? My husband's job was secure but not especially lucrative. To dream of a dazzling increase in pay was absurd. My job, in which I had been increasingly restive and dissatisfied, provided about half the household income. Should one of us find a higher-paying job? Who would hire a woman already pregnant? The future should have looked bleak. But the joy I discovered in that second (surprise!) pregnancy was unpredictably overwhelming. There was no room for financial worry. Amazed at myself, I realized that growing as steadily as the child in my womb was a desire to stay home and care for it myself. I wanted to experience the joy of this child for as many moments of its first days, its first years, as I could.

Granted, my job situation contributed to my desire for such a change. I was bored and frustrated. I'd spent four years going over other people's manuscripts, ferreting out errors which authors did not like called to their attention. I wanted to produce more of my own manuscripts, not just occasionally as spare time allowed, but without the handicap of my nine-to-five job.

Soon I would be thirty. I couldn't imagine myself a suburban housewife, a stay-at-home diaper changer. But the office I was in, or another one like it, was not the place I wanted to spend the rest of my life. Could God be using my biological clock to teach me about myself, to make my thirtieth birthday and the imminent birth of my second child a bench mark? Could I be changing? Were my values changing? Was this my personal Sturm und Drang, my own revolt against society's expectations of me? My place? Surely that particular office role could not be it. My purpose? I had no idea. Over and over the arguments within me continued. I agonized over them with sympathetic friends. I talked them over with my pastor. I discussed them with my husband.

Clearly, in a household organized and operating under a double income, such monumental decisions require the support of both partners. I had it. For me to do what I wanted, my husband Jack would have to stall his own career. He had recently completed law school and passed the bar examination. An attorney's position was the next logical step for him. But attorneys are not exactly scarce where we live—

Washington, D.C. To take a beginning attorney's position or start his own practice would mean a drastic drop in pay (meaning this book might be about living on a quarter of your/our income!). We had to choose. Either I went back to work (probably to the same place) after the baby's birth, while Jack tried his wings, or he must stick it out in his similarly dissatisfying job while I stayed home to write and change diapers (mostly change diapers). There was no hesitation, no waver in Jack's decision. It was my turn, he insisted, my opportunity.

Thus my new "employment," our new venture, was decided.

There wasn't a backlog of savings. We had not been conscientious about putting money away. We'd always intended to, but what we had we spent, assuming there could not be a day any rainier. Law school had not been cheap, though Jack had attended a night program so he could work days. For five years we'd been financially tied up in the restoration of an old wreck of a house. Mortgage payments were low, but taxes and new plumbing and all the rest of it were killers.

Looking back (and of course what they say about hindsight is true), I see all kinds of financial resources that trickled into nothing. Did I need a new pair of boots each year? Did my relatives expect such unnecessarily lavish gifts at holidays? Did I need so many magazines? Did I need to buy my skirts and Jack's ties at Brooks Brothers? No denying it, there had been extravagances.

And even earning money cost money. Office gifts. Stockings (it's surprising the tab hosiery can run up in a year). Child care. After-school child care for our daughter JC, then four, cost some two hundred dollars per month. Pre-school was extra.

In many ways it was humorous. My job was an editorial one on a magazine based on finance: how to get money, how to keep money, how to spend money, how to save money. Money, money, money. There I was, making sure the financial advice we gave to other people, John and Jane Q. Public, was correct, when I couldn't even manage my own purse. Many was the payday lunch hour I frantically dashed to the bank to cover checks which might not wait until five o'clock. Most of my knowledge amounted to academic exercise. I left it at the office.

My parents would have been dismayed. It's not for their lack of example that I'm just now learning about money. They'd always been circumspect, faithful stewards. There never had been much, but there was always plenty. That is, there had never been a question of money being available if it was needed. Theirs, my father's especially, was the plenitude that comes from frugality. Brooks Brothers? Izod alligators? The only label he recognized was Montgomery Ward. Dinner out was family fish night at Howard Johnson's. Yet our travels were the envy of everyone who knew us. By the time I was twelve I'd visited Mexico, Canada, Europe, and every continental state but one.

"How do they do it?" I heard folks whisper enviously behind my parents' backs. Those people didn't know the many nights we turned tired eyes toward the inviting lights of a motel vacancy sign, only to have my father return from the manager's office to our car. Eight dollars was too much for a night's rented bed. We went on until we found one for five. Pennies counted. There were no potato chip crumbs in our car; there were no potato chips. That money would buy us a few more miles of gas. I try to remember this when I'm tempted by the Wheat

Thins in my own grocery. A similar sum represents a gallon of gas. Eight of them are all it takes to get us to the beach and back.

And they tithed. Just before my tenth birthday, my father called me into his study where he sat behind the desk upon which I now write. He wanted to talk to me about money. The amount of money and the source of it I've long forgotten, along with the details of our conversation. But the money he talked about was mine, and the object of our discussion was tithe. He neither defined it nor gave me a pep talk on its merits. I'd been raised in a Christian home, and I was not stupid. Ten years of example was, presumably, enough of a lesson; he did not need to articulate it further. My father intended this to be a bench mark. The money was mine. I, being of an accountable age and educated enough in mathematics to figure out ten percent, was to mark my coming birthday by my first tithe. That's how he had marked his, embarking on a lifelong habit. It was my last tithe for nearly twenty years.

There are books and books and books on tithing. The stories, the few I've read, are thrilling and sometimes incredible. More incredible is the thought of one's *own* check going into the offering plate! I don't claim to understand why, but the thrill is also greater. Last Ash Wednesday I watched, eyes wide, as a friend summoned all her will and wrote out a check for tithe she considered overdue. Her hands trembled. Mine trembled more. If mine is a shoestring budget, there is no defining hers. She is single, doing free-lance work, eeking out a living from week to week, trusting that the next job will be there when she completes the current one. To put it mildly, she has neither independent wealth nor a backlog of waiting jobs. It's she who waits. Usually the job's not there until the very moment she completes the one she's on, but there's always *a* job which covers the bills if she takes care not to accumulate needless ones.

With me, it seemed there was never enough to tithe. Those volumes of tithing stories always seemed to feature folks who could afford it: entrepreneurs of vast means, wealthy heiresses, prosperous professionals for whom it was not a sacrifice but a spiritual principle. Or else they were the poorest of the poor, with "few obligations anyway." Certainly they weren't stories of a young and struggling parent like myself, trying to beat the overwhelming financial odds of life in middle-income America. A tenth of nothing is nothing. Maybe when I got some extra money?

So I was given some extra money. Actually I earned it. I sold an extra story, but I was still on payroll so I had to admit it was extra. My opportunity had arrived. Would I or wouldn't I? I did. I tithed it and immediately sold another story. I tithed again. This wasn't so bad. I started tithing payroll money, not my husband's but my own. Still not so bad. Then came the big one, my last check from my employer, my share of deferred profit-sharing, the sign-off given to every departing employee. It was going to be our cushion during many a "half-of" income month. I literally closed my eyes as I released the tithe of it into the offering plate. Have we been blessed with mind-boggling spirals of financial fortune? Hardly. I have a few spellbinding stories, but hardly a bookful. But I *do* have peace of mind and heart and the assurance that our immediate *needs* will somehow be met.

Do I still yearn for scads of money? Sometimes. Would I tithe it? Absolutely. Would I then have a book for that library? Not unless I discover and take to heart those secrets of humility.

If there was any question as to whether we had *quuuiiiite* pared down to half our income by the time the idea for this book was gestated, there's no question now. I live on faith and frugality (more of the second, to be honest). But we are doing what I never thought we could. Do I want to do it indefinitely? OUCH! I want to say yes, but in honesty I must put it this way:

My hat goes off to people who decide, for either ethical or Christian reasons, that they must pare down to the simplest of existences forever. My choice was neither so altruistic nor long-range. It wasn't the desire for a simpler, less money-oriented lifestyle that prompted this year or two or three away from an office. The prompting was my desire for different circumstances, more fulfillment, come what may financially. The "prompter" I realized only later, was divine. God intends to meet every need of both me and my family. That includes my need to fulfill the dreams He has put in my heart as well as whatever talent He has placed in my hands or head. Those needs, I have realized, I am unable to fulfill on my own, though I spend a lifetime striving. Only as I follow His direction are they satisfied.

2

Salvation Sally
or
Secondhand
Rose?

"It's no good, it's no good!"
says the buyer;
then off he goes
and boasts about
his purchase.

PROVERBS 20:14

My sister, mother of two by the time I was born, abhors anything that whispers "used." She grew up, as did I, in a parsonage chock-a-block with vestiges of Victoriana: heavy, somber artifacts only recently again in vogue. In my sister's youth they were mere castoffs, too ratty for the congregation but good enough for the preacher's family. By the time the much younger child—me—reached the age where such things mattered, the family's financial situation had changed, but few of the furnishings had been replaced. "Used" was now a matter of choice, not necessity. The difference in our childhoods resulted in opposite adult attitudes.

To this day, my sister would rather sit on the floor than accept someone's discarded settee. She'd wear the same outfit week in, week out before she'd wrap her body in a thrift-shop suit. At the slightest indication of wear, out it goes, whatever "it" may be: towels, furniture, clothes, kitchenware, books, carpets. Her house and her person are clean, spare, orderly, new. She may have little that is top of the line, but she has nothing that smells of secondhand rose.

I veer to the other extreme. My nature is that of the confirmed packrat. I throw out none of the dusty and musty; indeed, I go out of my way to acquire it. One might be forgiven for mistaking our house for a secondhand shop. My idea of paradise is a lusty country auction. I revel in an afternoon's ramble through a neighborhood of junk stores and thrift shops. My pulse quickens when I espy a lawn sale. Certain telltale trash piles cause my stomach to flutter.

Obviously, my sister and I don't enjoy shopping together. I seldom go to Sears with her, and she never tags along on my excursions to the Salvation Army. But we're exactly alike when it comes to controlling *how much* we spend. Our shared heritage has made us alike in that respect.

Restraining myself to secondhand stuff is not usually a painful sacrifice. But restraint in itself is. I could bargain myself into bankruptcy. Why do I need a seventh, oak-trimmed, beveled mirror? Five winter coats? So many books even the closets overflow with them? My rationale is that I can get this—too!—because it's secondhand. I'm just now understanding that God has provided my preference for secondhand roses as an opportunity for me to save money, not squander it. I'm just now realizing that I should acknowledge these things as coming *instead*, not *in addition*. Through my greedy inability to pass up unneeded bargains, I've denied my family many rightfully deserved comforts of life. They, for instance, would gladly trade a room's worth of uncomfortable gewgawed walnut for one comfortable, feet-on couch.

Most important in the list of caveats for secondhand shoppers is: Buyer, beware of *yourself*! A bargain is not a bargain unless you need it, can afford it, and would be buying a comparable item in the foreseeable future anyway.

Rationalization is every insatiable shopper's nemesis. In my closet hang five winter coats. With the exception of one Sunday, I wore exactly one—a camel jacket—all winter long. It's comfortable. It looks good. It goes with everything. I like it. What about the four others? One's too short, another's too long, the third's the wrong color, and the fourth makes me look heavier than I like to think I am. But hems can be altered, seams adjusted. Color, of course, is not easily changed; but if I liked the shade once, might I not like it again sometime? True, the camel jacket I wore every day last winter cost four dollars. True, it's been nearly eight winters since I bought the coat of the wrong color. True, I paid only twenty dollars for the one that's too short. The Harris tweed that's too long? Well, it was a *steal* at 75 percent off. But, "I need something else" was my rationale for purchasing every one of those coats!

Greed. We hoodwink ourselves by calling it need.

Take, for instance, the set of six Art Deco cups and saucers displayed in the front window of my local thrift shop last week. Four dollars! Wow! A fancy catalog I'd recently sighed over featured similar ones, thirty-dollar reproductions of these, the genuine article. It must be that I was intended to have them. I nearly convinced myself; we entertain a lot and we have no proper after-dinner coffees. Never mind that I gave away two entire sets as a foolish young bride. Never mind that these weren't quite what I'd had in mind for proper after-dinner coffees. These would do until I found the ones I really wanted. And then I'd get those too? I walked home to my mugs.

How many lessons does it take? Some are as dull as a pair of shoes, as frivolous as a silk scarf. A few days later I was in that same shop and found three pairs of shoes, a dollar per pair, I could use. The first I put back, self-congratulatory; they were a duplicate of some I already own which still have several miles of leather left. The second wasn't so easy. The fit was not quite perfect, but they were seventy-dollar shoes and practically unworn. The third I kept: colorful designer sandals of canvas. They felt like a cushion and cost a quarter. So proud I was "taking no heed lest I fall," I turned toward the cash register. Ahhh! A bin of silk scarves. Only seventy-five cents each. I bought one of course—despite the fact that it is a shape I never use and a shade that matches nothing I own. I've felt guilty ever since, my delight in my sandals spoiled.

● ● ●

But greed disguised as need isn't always attracted to such nonessential niceties as after-dinner coffees or silk scarves. It can be as banal as children's pajamas or end-of-inventory cocktail napkins. The "essential nutrients" thrift shops provide at low cost can become a sweet sort of poison if you overdose.

But they can be sustenance. Looking good is part of feeling good. You don't have to *appear* poor or tasteless. The camel jacket for which I paid four dollars and wore literally every day last winter is of superb quality. It might have cost close to a hundred full retail, probably half that even at the end-of-season sale. It wasn't new, but what is, once the price tag is removed? All it needed was a dry cleaning and leather buttons to make it far more handsome than a new-but-sleazy counterpart from some discount department store. So I grabbed it when I saw it, part of the secret to shopping secondhand successfully, whether at thrift shops, consignment shops, lawn sales, or flea markets. If it's an attractive bargain, it will move fast.

If you find something good near the top of a bin, it's only because you got to it before anyone else. It was probably just put there. Quality merchandise moves faster and faster these days, as more people establish new cost-cutting shopping habits.

THRIFT SHOPS

Thrift shops are becoming busy places, but if you are to use them wisely and well, consider the following tips.

You may spot bargains in season or out. My little gem of a jacket I found hidden away, one steamy August afternoon, behind several dozen dowdy dresses better sold to the ragman. The canvas sandals came on a February day, after a five-minute dig through leather and vinyl (mostly vinyl) deserving only of a child's dress-up collection.

Bargains often need minor repairs, and few of them come in perfect condition. You get your good deal because someone else was too lazy or too unimaginative to make good use out of what is now yours. Sixty-dollar shoes may only need sixty cents worth of laces or new lifts for the heels. Because one button was missing, I had to buy a complete new set for my camel jacket. But I would have anyway; the prior owner had replaced whatever buttons were original with some garish substitutes. A yellow leotard with attached tutu I bought for my five-year-old's birthday required a long soak and five minutes with my needle and thread. A similar leotard, new, would have cost twelve dollars. Hers cost two. Heavy cabled tights retail for approximately six dollars; the average price for a secondhand pair is under a dollar. All I have to do is sew up the inevitable hole in the toe.

A bargain isn't a bargain if it can't or won't or doesn't get fixed. I've bought nothing that can't be fixed, but we have a houseful (or so my husband will testify!) of bargains that need "a little attention."

Thrift shop policy generally is "take it as it is." Guarantees and return policies are virtually nonexistent. Store credit is the most you can hope for if you find a surprise (bad fit, poor color match, stain, crack) when you get home. But don't expect anything.

Scrutinize spectacular buys. Those apparently perfect specimens may be irregulars that slipped past some chagrined buyer's eye earlier at the retail level. They may be unacceptable to you for the same reason the original buyer discarded them. Check zippers, buttons, fit, plaids and prints (mismatched or upside-down), sleeves, and linings. Dim lighting hides a multitude of flaws, so carry the item to doorway daylight (or outside, if they'll let you) to look for tiny spots, large stains that blend in, fronts and backs cut from two slightly different bolts of the same cloth, and other irregularities. Check chairs for broken springs, tables for splitting wood. Abandoned late-model household goods (such as vacuum cleaners, blenders, or toasters) are likely to have some major fault. At the very least, plug them in. (Frayed wires can be fixed or replaced.)

Don't trust size labels on new or used goods. What started out as a size eight is likely to be closer to a six or four if it's worn. Unworn clothes are good bets for wrong labels, the very reason they may have been sold originally as "irregulars" and later discarded by the unsuspecting purchaser who thought the sale price a good deal.

Don't expect fitting rooms. You may not want to use the rare ones available anyway. To say some shops are cleaner than others is to say, euphemistically, some are not as dirty as others. Hard as some places try, it's impossible to win the battle against grime when grubby merchandise jostles sleeve-to-sleeve, neck-to-neck with the minority of squeaky-clean merchandise. Welcome to the egalitarian world of thrift shops! Hold your nose—figuratively of course—and shower when you get home. Try garments on over your own clothes (everybody does), then clean them thoroughly as soon as you get them home.

Instead of a list of sizes, carry a list of measurements for everyone you might buy for, and update it occasionally. I also keep a cloth tape measure in my purse, although most places have a measuring tape you can borrow.

For children, buy big, but remember what you've socked away for future seasons. This winter, her sixth, JC wore a Lord and Taylor duffle coat I bought for eight or nine dollars when she was two. (L & T sold this year's version for eighty dollars.) When I dug out the duffle in November, I discovered a forgotten, somewhat smaller coat I'd intended for *last* winter.

Inventory changes continually. I make it a point to check in at my favorite places whenever it's convenient, sometimes a couple of times weekly. That way, I take advantage of changes in price as well as merchandise turnover.

Pricing policies are unpredictable. They vary from day to day, shop to shop, clerk to clerk. My two favorite shops are typical. Favorite, because they're within walking distance of our house, around the corner from one another, and carry essentials we'd have to buy retail if we didn't find them there. Typical, because their pricing is so frustratingly variable, primarily because they rely on good-willed but unskilled volunteers.

The day I bought the shoes mentioned earlier, I bought girls' tights at the same shop. Then I visited the place around the corner. They had several tights in stock—no wonder, priced at two dollars per pair.

The three or four other items I looked at were similarly overpriced. No bargains that day! A few days later I noticed a two-for-one sale sign in their window: buy the higher-priced of two items and get the other free. (A good sale, but I prefer the "one dollar for all you can stuff into your bag" type.) A dollar a pair was not my idea of a steal, but new, heavyweight cabled tights are six dollars a pair. Someone else must have thought the same. The bin, overflowing only a few days earlier, now held only one pair, price tag missing. I carried the tights and a twenty-five-cent Givenchy scarf to the counter, prepared to pull out a dollar. The clerk, evidently new, paused a moment and then asked the other lady behind the counter, "What do we sell tights for, anyway?" "I can't remember," was the reply. "Check the price list." "Fifty cents," my astonished ears heard, just before I saw her nod—with no small amount of interest—toward my "free" scarf. "Where did you find *that?*"

Ah-haaaaa! Number one, there is a price list, whether or not items are individually marked. Number two, volunteers occasionally don't even know such a list exists. Number three, the "help" likes to skim the cream of the merchandise—only fair, since most volunteers at thrift shops receive little or no other compensation.

Expect chaos. Mere dishevelment may be a pleasant surprise. Neatness and order belong in aptly named "department" stores, which thrifts may try to resemble but don't. The tights I found in the second shop were in an appropriately labeled dishpan. Those in the first shop I found in a box of hats and woolen scarves. A basketful of men's ties hid the Givenchy scarf.

Check out the men's department. Men's clothing offers some of the best deals I've seen. Unfortunately, I have only one of my own to relate. About eight years ago my husband bought the roughest, toughest corduroy sports jacket imaginable. It's even survived an unintentional trip through the family laundry. The fit remains perfect. It cost four dollars and looks better today than the ninety-dollar one he bought new only a couple of years ago. His present job requires only slacks and a sports jacket, or I might have a few tales about custom-made, seven-dollar suits. The men's racks are full of them, the sleepers in the thrift shop business. I don't know what accounts for it. Is it the inconvenient shopping expedition? The fact that the typically blue-collar thrift shop clientele have little need for 100 percent wool worsteds? The problem of size? (Prosperous donors typically have large waistlines as well as fine taste in fabric. But tailors can make necessary adjustments.) Whatever the reason, $250 suits go for seven or eight dollars.

Get better deals by observing thrift shop etiquette. Thrift shop staff tend to be genuine do-gooders. This is their "soup-line" mission. While they understand that a customer needn't be on welfare lists to appreciate thrift shop bargains, their primary concern is customers who have no other option. Most staff accept professional antique scouts as a fact of life but resent dress-for-success types who haggle over dimes and quarters. Save your dickering for big-ticket items. (Offer twenty for a rug or bed marked thirty. They may come down to twenty-five.) Try to make your face a familiar and friendly one. The volunteers who staff one of my two favorite places are as ever-changing as the customers and inventory. But at the other shop, the lady overseer who doubles as chief clerk sees me every time I go in; I make sure of it. As a regular and friendly customer *and donor*, mine is the occasional privilege of suggesting that the price might be too high or requesting that she bend the "no layaways" policy long enough for me to get to the bank. Like most thrift shops, they accept no checks or credit cards.

CONSIGNMENT SHOPS

Consignment shops are not to be confused with thrift shops. Rare, here, are two-dollar drapes. Rarer still are dollar-fifty silk blouses. Bone china is not found plopped on the same shelf as jelly glasses and dime store dinnerware. But nervous novices more familiar with middle-class malls will find these places less unsettling than the somewhat lower-priced thrift shops.

Consignment shops, usually for-profit establishments, know that to justify their prices and attract traffic from their competition they can't look like a junk store. Merchandise is clean and organized; original price tags sometimes dangle side by side with the shop's. Fitting rooms are common. Seldom is the cream of the merchandise skimmed from the top. Pricing policy is well-established.

Two-for-one sales and similar clearance bargains are rare at consignment shops, but sixty or ninety-day reductions are common. After a piece of merchandise has been displayed for sixty or ninety days from the date marked on the tag, it begins an incremental series of markdowns, perhaps 10 percent for each thirty days it remains unsold. Occasionally you'll see items overdue for a markdown or just plain overpriced. Point this out to the management; you may get a deal. (For example, the two young mothers who run Kids Again sometimes price brand-name products higher than the deals a sharp eye might spy on a clearance table at a large department store.) Management may have relied on the high estimates given by a consignor with unreasonably high hopes.

The following chart shows how attractive consignment shopping can be. I compiled it last time I visited the children's consignment shop (Kids Again) in my neighborhood. When I left, my shopping bag held the items in the first list. (All items except the shape sorter were worn but needed no repairs; the shape sorter appeared to have never been used.) The second list indicates what I would have paid elsewhere.

Navy blue camp shorts (boys' size 6)	2.50
Red and white play shirt (boys' size 6)	3.00
Patent leather Maryjane shoes	
(girls' size 11)	2.00*
Baby shoes	1.50*
Fisher Price shape sorter	2.00
2 pr. terrycloth infants' panties (no stains)	.50
1 pr. plastic-and-terry training pants	.50
Total	$12.00
Tax	.48
GRAND TOTAL	$12.48

Carol Reed catalog	9.00
J.C. Penney catalog	4.99
J.C. Penney catalog	15.00
local shoe shop	9.00
local toy store	6.99
J.C. Penney catalog	4.29
local discount store	1.29
Total	$50.56
Tax	2.02
GRAND TOTAL	$52.58

*ninety-day half-price reduction

Individuals aren't the only consignors. Businesses often consign or donate goods they can't unload elsewhere. Everybody benefits from this, especially when the goods are donations. The donor gets a tax deduction; the management can offer tempting prices; the buyer gets what amounts to a steal.

Recently an interior decorator near us plastered telephone poles with last-minute invitations to a one-day-only moving sale. It came and went too fast for most of us who might have attended had we been given earlier notice and longer opportunity, but when I stopped in at their new location to inquire about leftovers, the owner told me he'd sent everything to a charity consignment shop nearby. There were ten- to forty-dollars-per-yard remnants and samples, each one now priced at $1.50 per yard to simplify bookkeeping and move them fast. An effective ploy! When I went back the afternoon of the day of my discovery, the place was cleaned out. But on the spot that morning I spent about ten dollars and walked out with two hundred dollars worth of badly needed upholstery fabric. (True to my nature, I also wasted five dollars on irresistible hand-screened samples of no particular use.)

Consignment offers an opportunity to profit from your own mistakes, too. Clothes that no longer fit, duplicate gifts, surplus or disliked household paraphernalia: salvage part of their value by selling them through a consignment shop. They'll fetch a higher price than at a lawn or garage sale, but you must split cash-register receipts (probably 50–50) with the shopkeeper. You may also have to pay a small fee. The children's consignment shop near us charges two dollars, good for a year. Some shops charge a fee every time you carry in a load. Consignment entails risks. What if your goods become stained or broken while in the shop? What if they won't sell? Who sets prices? Shop policy varies, so discuss these questions with the management *before* you make your appointment to consign anything of great value.

LAWN AND GARAGE SALES

Few activities satisfy as thoroughly as lawn or garage sales, either as sponsor or shopper. They've displaced flea markets in my affections, now that flea markets are basically another way to spell A-N-T-I-Q-U-E. Not that I've suddenly acquired a dislike for antiques. But when I have to scratch for pennies to keep my legs in run-less stockings, walnut whatnots and porcelain baubles appear as absurd as they really are. Flea markets were fun when they were an eclectic group of farmers and small-time peddlers out to make a nickel, but most are now mere havens for every mavin out for a quick buck. If you're lucky enough to live in an area where the old-time type flea market still exists, enjoy. But most of us will have to settle for lawn or garage sales.

Not that these don't have their share of hucksters. I'm wary of any sales that appear to be more than a few days old. After that, either the good stuff's gone or the homeowner apparently listing away in the aluminum lawn chair is really a mercantile magnate scheming to turn his or her driveway of discards into a grand emporium.

Never mind. The educated miner still finds gems sparkling through the riffraff and overpriced trinkets. At one of those lawn sales where jelly glasses were going (*not* going, actually!) for a dime apiece, I found a box off to the side, its entire junky contents priced at fifty cents. Jumbled among its peanut butter jars and plastic spoons were eight unblemished juice glasses straight out of the thirties. They are now the inspiration of many a conversation when guests sit at our breakfast table. Their cost? A nickel each.

On the same lawn I found six Victorian curtain rods, fluted wood with spirally brass tips, the type now reproduced in plastic and peddled for several dollars each in department stores. They were bound together with adhesive tape that also served as the price tag—seventy-five cents. We needed curtain rods; I bought them.

The best lawn sales are those you happen upon. But who can afford the car fuel for that kind of weekend drive on a regular basis? And if you see one en route to a destination, there's usually no time to linger. But a planned sale visit is better than none at all. For me, it relieves the tension that accumulates if I don't get a chance to indulge my primeval instinct for haggling. Who cares if it's over a fifteen-cent toilet brush? My favorite information sources are the local (usually weekly) advertising newspapers of tiny circulation. Low circulation limits competition, and county maps help you locate gold mines, usually way off the beaten track. Most folks don't bother. Those who do are the professional antiquers, but what they leave is still plenty good enough for the rest of us.

"Cash for trash" trills one headline after another from the magazine racks beside grocery checkouts. There's even a book on the subject. But don't squander your potential profits. A half-dozen common-sense guidelines—and some experience as a customer—are all you need.

Advertise. Anyplace free—telephone poles, bulletin boards at the grocery or library or nearest unemployment office or anyplace else where people stand around, church bulletins, school newsletters —is good. An ad or two in a newspaper also makes good sense. Offer more information than time and place. Note categories and specific, enticing items: auto supplies, VW tires, electric typewriter, baby clothes, women's size 8 clothes, used furniture including antique desk, kitchenware including pressure cooker, etc. Make your signs large and clear.

Put your telephone number on the advertisement. People may be tempted by your ads but may want more precise information to make a trip worthwhile.

Wear something with large, heavy-duty pockets. Neat little money boxes are charming and show your organization. But one, they're easily stolen or picked through; and two, once things start to roll you won't have time to sit quietly behind your little table. If it's a successful sale, you'll be in three or four places at once answering questions and making change.

Have lots of small bills and change ready. If you accept checks, require at least two forms of identification—and write down the appropriate (telephone number, credit card, ID, address) information!

If yours is a cooperative venture, make sure everything is properly marked as to owner. Another method, which simplifies bookkeeping when customers select items from several different sellers, is agreeing to split the kitty at the end. Money mix-ups can harm otherwise friendly relationships, and financial confusion is invariable at a rapidly paced sale. So be forewarned and prepared.

If you're willing to consider all offers, put up a sign to that effect.

Whether you mark items individually or by

grouping, keep a master price list. Honest customers understand that items become "mislaid."

Leftovers? Don't throw them out for a day or two. Someone may have second thoughts about an unmade purchase. Or someone may make an offer on everything that's left. A lady I know did this at every area sale for one whole summer. She spent a pittance and relieved the homeowners of a clean-up job. Around Labor Day she sponsored a sale of her own and made a thousand dollars! Another possibility is to drop the leftovers off at a charity organization and take the tax deduction.

My first lawn sale was also the first in the rural community where we lived. It being 1973, one didn't see similar sales on every corner or articles about them in every magazine. I was a little nervous. I coaxed my good friend and neighbor, Joy, into cooperating. By cleaning their closets one morning, her two kids tripled the inventory it had taken Joy and me two weeks to assemble. But her kids were *nothing* compared to Joy's husband. He ha-ha'd and pooh-pooh'd our project the whole time we planned it and well into the sale—right up to the moment somebody laid down fifty dollars for Joy's old dishwasher that had sat in the garage for several years. Ron then hit the garage, cellar, and attic. He emptied dusty bookshelves and halved his record collection. He has moaned ever since about how much he could have gotten for his old tools, if only he'd had them out for the early rush!

ESTATE SALES

Seldom do I take advantage of this highbrow, "inside" sort of lawn sale. (When we need more furniture, I will.) Prices are seldom bargain-basement variety. Ordinarily a professional is called in to organize and to price goods, usually of premium quality. Because they're "in the business," it's not unusual for these professionals to let their cronies have first pick. But this is the place to find chafing dishes of copper or silver as well as odds and ends of fine china. (Heirs of the deceased or the organizer's cronies usually take full sets of crystal or china, fine antiques, and valuable art.) Rugs and furniture are excellent bargains because part of the purpose of the sale is to avoid the expense of storing or moving a houseful of cumbersome goods. If you don't see items you're interested in, ask. Sometimes what you might want is the very thing the organizer was sure no one would care about.

SURPLUS AND HOTEL RENOVATION SALES

I've never used surplus sales, and I've used hotel renovation sales only once. We had to replenish our pillow supply, and the hotel pillows were clean in spite of being dirt cheap. That particular sale was advertised in the classifieds, but most are not. In fact, you have to inquire because most sales are totally informal. The best procedure is to contact the person in charge of housekeeping at your local lodging place, (not the chambermaid, but the manager). Ask how often they refurbish. At busy places, it may be as often as every two years. When they do, beds, blankets, bureaus, draperies, lamps, towels, and anything else you find in a lodging place may become available for a song.

Surplus sales are trickier. The best policy is to keep an eye on the classifieds, as they are usually advertised. Sometimes the bidding is for huge quantities or is "sealed," meaning, in effect, you're at an auction. Check the following chapter on auctions, particularly the section on government auctions.

TRASH PILES (?!?!?)

Then there's garbage. For years antiquers have been smart enough to roll up their shirt-sleeves and hit the dump, where the best pickings are to be found. My neighborhood alleys keep me busy! Not that I scrounge the cans: propped beside them are hassocks and brass lamps (yes, solid!) and silver trays and rugs and bookcases and wooden wardrobes. Every one of these items I have personally snatched from the jaws of the hungry machine that rumbles through Tuesday mornings at seven o'clock sharp. Every item is now in use, except the hassock, which even I, on closer look, had to admit was a goner. Granted, we live in a neighborhood where the cars (all but ours) parked next to the trash are Mercedes or Volvos or some such. Trash reflects income. But even here I find Rubbermaid dish drainers (probably the color was wrong).

Yet I'm not the only scavenger. It always shocks me to find my own trash has walked off. Mine! Filtered through the ultimate scavenger—me—my trash is *trashy!* Who could possibly want it? Obviously somebody does.

Yes, scavenging can be embarrassing. But you need not be mistaken for a ragpicker. I've been known, after spotting something desirable but in a public place, to dash home and change my clothes—to something better—before I drag off my trophy. Only a couple of times has this pride been a problem. I've dashed back to the garbage site to claim my booty, only to discover someone's beaten me to it!

3

Don't Scratch Your Nose

*A fool's mouth is his
undoing,
and his lips are a snare
to his soul.*

PROVERBS 18:7

Compared to the bonanzas of the good old days of a decade or two ago, today's auction prices seem outrageous. But they aren't, I realize every time I allow myself the pleasure of an auction. They are, in fact, irresistible.

I caught auction fever as a youngster, when my dollar bid at Rigsbee's Auction Barn was the winner on a camelback trunk, its jammed lock safeguarding enchanting treasures from each of the last dozen decades. I still revel in the memory of my delighted discovery, especially when I spot the price tags attached to items like those I found in the trunk, now long gone but most of its contents carefully preserved.

As student newlyweds, our household budget made auctions (lawn sales were not yet common) the only plausible source of household goods. Estate and household auctions were fun and profitable, but farm auctions were bliss. Bidding farmers fought furiously over pigs and tractors—and literally *gave* me enough stuff to furnish not only our house, but residences of several similarly impoverished friends, with everything from dishpans to crazy quilts to canning jars to country oak. At that time, now-popular oak was leftover, undesirable hand-me-down junk stuck out in the back shed to hold rusty tools and old string. Auction after auction, Saturday after Saturday, farmer after amused farmer saw this quaint young female cramming their discards into her rusty VW. "Honey, you look like you might want a little of this, now. Help yourself." So I did. I grabbed whatever they threw and sorted back home. Neither the farmers nor I realized, then, the value of their largess. They do now. Similar auctions today are full of lynx-eyed antique "pickers" and wary farmers.

Auction prices, like prices in general, change. But when I go to an auction, it all rushes back. The bargains are different. No longer am I offered free brass beds or walnut commodes. Neither do I bid on them. I focus, as I did when the brass beds were giveaways, on what is unpopular. And I still walk away with bargains.

This year it was rugs.

The living room of the house we'd been restoring for five-years-plus had a thirty-foot expanse of just-refinished hardwood floor daring us to scratch it. We adapted by leaving our shoes by the doorway, Japanese-style. But what about guests? I shopped those carpet discount warehouses, where fifty or one hundred dollars gets a room-size remnant. None seemed suitable. What I *wanted* was a nine-thousand (at least!)-dollar Oriental for $99.99. But I didn't find it. Finally, at a clearance sale, I located what I thought might partially solve the problem. It wasn't the Oriental, of course, but it was wool, dense, of classic Grecian design. I wavered. The color tone was close but not perfect, and it was big enough for only a third of the problem area. But the price cinched it. Originally eight hundred, the rug was reduced to two hundred dollars. I would get it the next week after our trip to upstate New York, home of my farmer auctions.

That October Saturday in New York was perfect for an auction—chilly air and threatening clouds; fair-weather gadflies who up my humble bids stayed home. That thinned the competition for what were great pickings. The son of the village's deceased judge was ridding himself and his heirs of several decades worth of the rural heritage that his new and savvy urban life would not accommodate. Walnut side chairs went for twelve dollars a pair, with no one in the audience with vision to see beyond the rip in the leather of the horsehair-stuffed seats. Nor could anyone (but myself and the clever buyer) see past the admittedly hideous pictures framed in hand-carved woods. Without pictures, in many city shops or galleries the frames might go for fifty dollars each. The glass alone was worth the three or four dollars most fetched that afternoon.

Here and there, throughout the house, rugs and carpets were rolled or wadded. There was no way to examine them properly. By mid-afternoon, time for us to leave, none had yet been brought to the auctioneer's block on the front porch. So I marched into the house through an open back door (There's always a sign that says not to enter, but if you have specific business you'll be forgiven *if* the crowds have thinned. Just don't undertake a meandering examination of the contents without permission.) I lugged some rugs to a spot near one of the auctioneer's assistants. "Can you do these soon?" I asked. "Sure thing," he replied, and within fifteen minutes a rolled rug was brought to the block.

"Three!"
"Four!"
"Five!"
"Six!"

Back and forth the bidding went—too quickly. I panicked, but it stopped abruptly at "Nine!" I couldn't believe it. The rug, the little I could see of it, appeared to be worn but of good wool and classic design. It would go for at least fifty, maybe eighty, in a decent consignment shop. But it was mine for nine! I lugged it to the side yard. It was considerably heavier than it appeared. No wonder! When I unrolled it, I discovered four more rugs inside! My nine dollars had purchased a genuine Oriental, two American imitations, and two patterned broadlooms —all of wool.

Should you think my rug purchase just a fluke, an error on the auctioneer's part, let me add that, that afternoon I also bought two eight-inch crystal candlesticks and a similar one of pressed glass for a total of seven dollars. An oak parson's table cost me thirty-seven dollars. (I was "had," heady from the rugs).

Auctions aren't only for those who prefer aged artifacts. Nor are they for the timid. There are all kinds of auctions, all kinds of merchandise, but only one kind of successful bidder—spunky. You needn't be noisy or aggressive. The lowest winning bids often go to people who wait quietly, inconspicuously. But they're in there, sure of what they want. At least they make the auctioneer think so. (Maybe that temporary elation of derring-do explains why auction·fever runs so high.) Bidders must beware of themselves as much as anything or anyone else. That's the cardinal rule of a successful gambit into the auction market. There are other, lesser guidelines:

Prudent bidders check over the inventory before the sale. The items listed in the auction's announcement you spot on a bulletin board or in the newspaper or penny-saver weekly are usually but the tip of the iceberg. At my kind of auction this means arriving twenty minutes or so before showtime. The whole thing's quite informal. But this is only true of most farm or country auctions. Some farm or country auctions and other general merchandise auctions and most estate auctions set up a viewing time, perhaps over a period of several days, in the week preceding the auction. Nearly all catalog auctions, so named because pre-auction inventory booklets are available, operate this way. Be sure to snoop through boxes and bureaus. They're sometimes sold unopened. (Remember my camelback trunk?) And I know of one woman who picked up a genuine pearl brooch, à la Queen Victoria, this way.

Sometimes there's an admission fee. I usually avoid this type, as they're either catalog auctions or fund-raisers for charity. Both types usually exceed my price range and probably yours, if you're reading this seriously. Old-time auctions (most before *my* time!) were simple undertakings. When you took the bid you paid—anonymously, in cash and on the spot—the auctioneer's helper who delivered your purchase. No more. Before you're allowed in the door, you present identification and, at some auctions, evidence of good credit. Some auctions accept only cash or traveler's checks or certified checks as payment. Sign-in complete, you're given a numbered card or paddle; then it's up to you to find a seat. Sometimes when you make—and *always* when you take—a bid, you wave your number so the auctioneer's bookkeeper can keep track of who must pay for what.

The auctioneer opens the bidding by setting a price which is probably the minimum acceptable. He (sometimes she) hopes that's the bidding floor, not the ceiling. But if nobody responds to the auctioneer and if the atmosphere is informal, you can holler out a lower offer. ("Five!" for instance, if the auctioneer's been trying unsuccessfully for ten.) You may receive snickers or frowns. Who cares? You may get the item—and the attentive eye of the auctioneer for the rest of the day. Auctioneers realize time is money; five quick dollars may be preferable to ten slow ones. You may become a favorite bidder for whom the auctioneer "knocks down" (sells fast at a low price) to speed up the auction.

My husband loves to relate the time, soon after our wedding, I made a rare visit to a catalog auction. Jack arrived with our coffee just in time to drag me away from four dozen pieces of French crystal that were going for "only" nine dollars each. That represented 432 dollars of college tuition. I had thought the bid was by the dozen! The lesson: **Know whether the bid is for each (by the piece) or for the whole group (by the lot).** Auction catalogs should specify this information. If there's no catalog, the auctioneer makes an announcement either before the auction begins or as each item comes to the block.

The traditional "Going, going, gone!" is itself almost gone. Occasionally you'll hear it, but more often it's a more abrupt "Sold!" Don't expect a hammer either, although the "Sold!" or "Gone!" you hear represents the "hammer price." After that, it's yours. Until that final moment, don't be intimidated by the auctioneer. If you're confused or if you've lost track in the fast stutter that auctioneers often use, don't hesitate to ask or signal "My bid?" or "What price?" Shyness can be expensive!

Each auction has its own good values. General merchandise or estate auctions are good sources for bargains if you need bulky pieces of furniture that are used but not antique. Broadloom carpets can be had for a song almost anywhere, as synthetic fibers and new wall-to-wall are more popular today. Sets of fine china and glassware are good deals if you compare their prices to comparable new ones and if your budget allows such luxuries. Some of the best deals come early at auctions held at private homes. Before the auctioneer ascends the block, he cleans out the garage or back shed. I've seen power mowers go for five dollars, radial saws for thirty, a bushel basket of garden tools pull in no more than a dollar. Why? Perhaps bidders are not yet in the swing, perhaps the few people on hand for auction startups are saving their money for the "real" stuff. Whatever the type of auction, the best bargains are likely to be the unfeatured items (like linens at an auction featuring farming equipment or tools and lumber at an auction monopolized by antique devotees).

GOVERNMENT AUCTIONS

Then there's the other, "hidden" world of government auctions. Discovering them is somewhat more complicated than glancing through your local papers, although government auctions occasionally are listed in the classifieds. Government at all levels—local, state, and federal—conducts auctions. Police and sheriff auctions vary by locality and are the most likely to be listed in the classifieds; check "sales" and "miscellaneous" as well as "auctions." Call your local police or sheriff department to find out how they handle dispersal of goods that might be sold at auction. Ask about pre-auction viewing, the expected number of viewers, and acceptable forms of payment.

Almost anything you can imagine—and a good deal you can't—is put on the block at one time or another by the U.S. government. Unfortunately, the pickings are unevenly distributed over both time and place because of what becomes available and the way the auctions are handled. Each agency handles the process differently.

The GSA (General Services Administration), through its Federal Supply Service, is the government's purchasing agent. They conduct four types of public sales or auctions, but only one is the traditional kind where you register and sit in a gallery to bid. Another is similar: bidders sit in a gallery but bid by written card (one chance only!) on items brought to the block. GSA's other two auction types are only appropriate for businesses which buy in huge quantities. Unless you're in a co-op that can use six dozen cots or the like, forget them. For more information, write to the GSA, Federal Supply Service, Personal Property Division at the GSA regional office nearest you. The federal government office listed in your telephone book can help you with the address. When you write, ask for *Buying Government Surplus Personal Property* and a mailing-list application. The first is a primer on rules and procedures. On the second you sign on for as many as you want of several dozen categories of upcoming sales. GSA also sells real estate, but not the kind of interest to most potential homeowners. Ask the GSA's regional Director of Real Property for information on "disposal of real property."

More interesting auction lots are offered by the customs offices and the postal service. Customs sells seized goods (who knows what you'll find!), odds and ends they label NCV (no commercial value), and appraisers' samples. The third category consists of items taken to establish import duty but not reclaimed, perhaps because their "loss" was figured into the importer's costs. Auction schedules and procedures (bidding and payment) vary from office to office. If you ask, you may be added to the mailing list (if they have one). For information on postal service auctions, call the Dead Parcel Branch. (The parcels are usually opened before being auctioned!) Some good deals from the postal service come in the form of vehicles. No longer needed, they're over-hauled before public sale. Contact the Postal Service Vehicle Maintenance Facility nearest you.

● ● ●

Auction fever must be nearing epidemic pro-portions. Every time I peruse the shelves of my neighborhood bookstores it seems there's an auction book hot off some willing victim's typewriter. So far, the best general-purpose introduction (also excelling in information on government sales) I've seen is *Cashing in on the Auction Boom* by James Wagen-voord, recently printed in paperback ($2.95) by Warner Books. Wagenvoord puts his finger on my response to auctions. He says they are theater! And I say, if you can't go to play a role, at least go and enjoy the show.

4

Sweat Equity Can Be Sweet

*The sluggard craves and
gets nothing,
but the desires of the
diligent are fully
satisfied.*

PROVERBS 13:4

Our home resembles those "What's wrong with this picture?" lessons my kindergartner brings home. Chairs without legs. Bureaus without bottoms. Settees without seats. Lamps without cords. Frames without pictures. Pictures without frames. Even a clavichord without keys. Our four walls reflect the forays—to auctions, barn sales, trash piles—mentioned in the preceding chapter.

My husband declares our next residence will have a barn as port-of-entry, through which all goods must pass for fumigation, renovation, and/or disposal. Neither his castle nor anything in it will so much as hint of a past or a present or—especially!—a future status as "handyman's special." Living in "reduced circumstances" is one thing. Quite another is trying to live—with any civility—among the clutter that constitutes our parlor-cum-workshop. "Grab it quick! We'll fix it later!" becomes a contagion, one against which my husband hopes to inoculate our new environs, should we ever reach them.

Maybe this year. . . . We've been saying that each year for the past six, the time it has taken to restore to its former glory, the DIY (do-it-yourself) way, the poor-man's Queen Anne we live in. Once again structurally firm and modestly regal, the house's sale should bring an attractive profit. We'll put it toward an already-complete domicile. And a barn.

Sweat equity. It's not for everybody. It's not for you if you can't tolerate disorder, if you aren't willing to relinquish relaxing weekends, if you value domestic tranquillity. The constant litter of ladders and lumber scraps tests marriages and tries friendships. Our house has cost us several friends (tempo-rary losses, I hope), not so much from ill will as from my hesitation to entertain amid the muddle. Dinner parties aren't a problem; candlelight hides any number of plaster bags and unplated light switches. Daylight is less kind. One doesn't encourage drop-in visitors who understand neither the mess nor the reason you can't leave a wall half plastered while you indulge in chitchat. House guests? Ha! Our mar-riage survived. Many don't.

If all this sounds frightening to you, you'd better stick with the small stuff. Projects as minor as covering a lampshade or replacing broken faucets. Projects as major as tiling a countertop or floor or paving a patio or rebuilding furniture. Home-maintenance repairs that must be made and that you, although a novice, can handle with a little help.

If you don't own a house but want to sometime, start furnishing it today. Rejuvenate other people's desirable discards now. When the big move comes, you won't be house poor: proud owner of walls and floor space but precious little else. Meantime, you brighten the corners where you are and, maybe, save money for a down payment. If your name's already on a deed but the mortgage leaves no room for fringes—like furniture!—fixing up goods you sal-vage for a pittance may be your almost-free ticket to the little comforts of life you'd understood were standard equipment in one's private castle.

Does this mean postponing plans for major home improvements—a new deck, a revamped kitchen, new furniture? Not necessarily.

Every project has two components—labor and materials. Most people pay with money. But you can't spend money you don't have. Even if you're foolish enough to consider your unemployed or low-income self a good risk for a loan, your banker isn't. Instead of trading labor and materials for your name on a dotted line, pay for your projects, large and small, with ingenuity and/or elbow grease, not necessarily in equal quantity.

Note the or between ingenuity and elbow grease. Perhaps you have lots of one and none of the other. If so, you're typical. If you wouldn't know where to begin with a large-scale project like a deck or a kitchen, find someone who does; then start to apply your own ingenuity. What can you do that the person who has the skills you need cannot do? Or, how can you reimburse a third party who, in turn, can reimburse the appropriately skilled second person? This is barter. (Read all about it in chapter 5.) Barter is the "poor" person's access to "unaffordable" goods and services.

So you've found a person with the skills to put your deck together or the people who can turn your culinary cubicle into a chef's delight. You still need materials. Barter again. Track down several sources. Unless they're in the business as professionals, few people can offer all the materials you need; and if they can, they may be in a position where they prefer cash. But lots of craftsmen and contractors have leftovers—not quite scraps but not worth their storage space. They may be happy to make a swap or to let you have the stuff in return for clearing their job site of what might otherwise be debris. Sometimes the materials are already on the scrap heap, either beside a construction site or a demolition project. You merely load your car.

We fixed a floor this way. A downtown office building was having its terra-cotta tile roof replaced. Terra-cotta tiles are heavy, and the roofer would not only have to discover a landfill site, but would have to pay laborers to load and unload several truckfuls. The solution? We offered to take them. We paid nothing, but we saved the roofer and ourselves a tidy sum. Comparable tiles would have cost us a couple of dollars each. Our cost, for 225 of them, was a tank of gas for the car and several sore muscles. We laid the tiles ourselves—a day's job for a professional, a three-weekend one for us. Our only cash expenses were cement and grout and an instruction book.

In similar fashion, we acquired bricks for our patio from a demolition site—several sites, in fact. Because of insurance complications in hard-hat areas, the workers hesitated to let me wander at will, so I had to content myself with bricks I could find near the fringe areas and at the convenience of the bulldozer driver. It helped that I made my visits during weekday lunch hours or in the evening when they had cleared out. First, the workmen didn't worry about me getting in the way of their monster machines. Second, they weren't threatened. What harm can a high-heeled lady who wants a "few" bricks do? Sometimes they 'dozed a load my way to make it easier for me to "fill" the car (little cars mean several little loads). My cost? Usually nothing. Sometimes a few cups of lemonade or coffee for the appreciative laborers. By using old bricks (including mismatches and half-bricks), we made our patio look as if it came with the house. It's rustic, to say the least! Laying it was a group effort. We bartered a picnic dinner for the help of our friends, novices all.

But bricks and tiles and a few friends do not an entire new kitchen make. If that's what you want, you may need to practice the salvage-and-barter routine, applying the first, second, and third-party principles many times over to obtain carpentry, plumbing, wiring, etc. Maybe you can swap your left-hand refrigerator for someone's right-hand one, your formica countertop for the services of a carpenter who'll make you a butcher-block replacement from scraps you scrounge from a lumbershop's trash bin. Will your old cupboards be suitable if they're merely rearranged (rehung)? What can you offer the person who'll help you move them? Perhaps a few custom-made party clothes for his/her youngster? Or if it's a willing and able retiree, how about their choice of pie each Sunday for the next year? What's it worth to you? This is do-it-yourself!

Then there's the do-it-yourself you do yourself. Our tile floor is an example. Most of the rest of our house is another. The bulk of the furnishings inside—the stuff for which my husband craves a barn!—are others. Rewiring lights is a cinch, the reason why I never pass by throw-outs. We have a dozen or so lamps and lighting fixtures still awaiting my attention. We have furniture . . . well, you read this chapter's first paragraph!

Acquiring projects is no problem. Storage and time can be. Do you have a garage, attic, basement, or barn? Our house, a city one, offers little storage space. A garage? What's that? We park our car in the alley, our bikes in my study. A heat pump occupies most of the attic. There is no basement. We make do. We live in crowded conditions, incorporating the to-be-fixed in with the finished. Sometimes this causes problems: keeping plants or otherwise out-of-character embellishments on chairs that would collapse if anyone tried to use them; explaining to quizzical guests why certain frames contain no pictures. But that does explain the stack of canvases they saw piled in a corner of the bathroom. So we've learned to live with our potpourri. After all, didn't someone say that variety is the spice of life? And variety we've got: tool chests stashed in kitchen cupboards, mirrors lining the bathroom wall, and . . . does anyone remember what's under that delicate table cover?

If space is a problem, you might partially solve it by acquiring only those things you enjoy working on. But if you have space to spare, save surplus "finds" for future barter—or a possible change of attitude.

Time is obviously as big a problem as lack of space. My "acquisition opportunities" arise in unequal (excessive) proportion to my fix-up time. Yours may be more in balance at first, depending on how sharp your eyes are, or your definition of irreparable, and on the value you place today on "needs" several years down the road.

WHAT TO FIX

Candidates for DIY projects are unlimited. Start exploring your own attic, basement, and closets. Especially plentiful usually are lamps and shades, unglued chairs, wobbly tables, and upholstered furniture. Initiate yourself with a simple project, such as framing artwork (everyone has something they are "going to have framed someday").

Anybody who hangs artwork on their walls (and who doesn't?) knows the cost of a frame can easily exceed the cost of its contents—whether a dimestore reproduction or a fine print or an original painting. One unpretentious solution: call a poster a poster a poster and, literally, pin it to the wall. But if it's fine enough to hang, it's fine enough to showcase. Even a free travel poster or a child's colorful scribbles assume an air of importance if well-matted and framed attractively. Unless you come into heirlooms from a well-heeled ancestor of excellent taste, you may, at least for the moment, need to make the most of those posters and scribbles, cartoons, old magazine covers, and dramatic fragments of fabric. A little art goes a long way if you frame it skillfully. A little money for framing goes a long way if you spend it shrewdly. Do-it-yourself can transform your bare walls and empty halls into stylish galleries.

Dimestore frames often suffice if you replace the ugly, flimsy mat. Thick, well-cut mat makes mediocre artwork and frames appear classier than they really are. Mat is inexpensive, and with a little practice you can produce first-class cuts: beveled edges and clean corners. You need a utility knife with several sharper-than-sharp blades, a straight edge (such as a yardstick that's firm and has no nicks), and several scraps of mat on which to hone your skills. One hint: always make your bottom border slightly deeper (wider) than the top one so bottom and top *appear* equal. A few frame shops cater to the DIY frames; they sell museum-quality, pre-cut mats at reasonable prices. Professionals cut mat for a small fee, but don't be conned into letting them frame your picture; you'll blow your entire art budget on one hanging! Those frame-it-yourself shops? One visit is not a bad idea for novices who can practice at home the techniques they learn at the shop.

Not any old frame will do for any old picture. You need to go to the trouble of making a good match, a problem if you don't tote your picture and mat with you when you shop for frames. One solution (mine): keep a selection of frames on hand (no great expense or trouble if you keep an eye peeled for throw-outs or auction bargains and don't mind storing them in the bathroom!). I have dozens of frames, all shapes and sizes and materials and dating from all "periods"—Empire, Victorian, Deco, Nouveau, Modern. Hint: For "primitive" art such as comes from the hand of a child, consider inexpensive and rough-looking building materials. The Corcoran, a prestigious art gallery in Washington, D.C., recently held a first-class show of primitive folk art. The framing was unsanded lathboard painted in "faded" shades of bright colors; nails were not only visible; they were part of the "art."

Picture Framing by Max Hyder ($2.95) costs about as much as a large sheet of museum-quality mat. This forty-seven page book covers all a novice needs to know about proportion, frame construction, mat, glass cutting, and assembly (putting art, mat, and liner into a frame). Hyder's book may be available in your local art supply shops. If not, you can save yourself the headaches many inferior texts have given me if you order the book directly from the publisher, Grosset & Dunlap in New York. The odds and ends of assembly materials the book enumerates (glue, brown wrapping paper, brad nails) are available in most dimestores.

Fix those objects that give you pleasure. Remember that DIY should be a labor of love! Jobs you detest seem to be delayed indefinitely, but jobs you enjoy may inspire an overflow. Use it to best advantage. An hour with a brass lamp (I've found them trashed because of a mere 85¢ broken switch!) and a couple dollars worth of replacement parts: you have a gift anyone should appreciate. An hour with a buzz saw, turning wood scraps into kindling: you do a favor (for Christmas perhaps) that will warm the cockles of a fireplace owner's heart, especially a city friend who has no back forty to scavenge. A day with a can of refinisher and a sturdy junkshop table: you have a prize present for a cherished friend or relative. (Give it to them without a finish; let them choose stain or oil or polyurethane or varnish which you later apply.)

Fix the broken or malfunctioning mechanical paraphernalia around your house or apartment. Avoid a fifty-dollar service call for what might be a two-dollar part. One large corporation with the resources and necessity for large-scale market research says that consumers now perform about 40 percent of their major-appliance repairs. That corporation, General Electric, has decided to capitalize on the trend. They now market a special line for do-it-yourselfers. Their "Quick-Fix" program—five manuals ($6.95 each) and 100 or so of the most-used repair parts ($2–$30) available in GE dealers' showrooms—is designed for GE appliances. But if the program is successful, other appliance manufacturers are bound to follow suit.

If your "to-be-fixed" is a plumbing problem, a real humdinger you can't solve, try "Geno," a toll-free hotline established by the Genova Co., a manufacturer of plastic plumbing supplies. Genova's experts offer free advice to homeowners Monday through Friday, 8:00 A.M.–5:00 P.M. (EST). Call 800-521-7488 from outside Michigan, 800-572-5398 from within that state.

Myriads of magazines publish articles to help the do-it-yourselfer. You don't need to subscribe. Visit your library and use the photocopier, or trade/share subscriptions with a friend.

Then there are the books, scads of them, for handy-homeowner types. They work for renters too. Books range from the general to the specific. A few are classics, the help they offer is so valuable. Two excellent all-purpose texts are published by Reader's Digest. Both *The Reader's Digest Complete Do-It-Yourself Manual* and *The Reader's Digest Fix-It-Yourself Manual* include step-by-step, illustrated instructions plus an explanation of how to use the appropriate tool. They are widely distributed and cost $19.95 each. A book that should be in every residence is *Do it Yourself and Save Money,* by the editors of *Consumer Guide* and published by Harper & Row. It costs $14.95 and is well-described by its subtitle, "500 things you've always had to pay other people to do for you."

Time-Life Books has produced an excellent series of volumes on home maintenance and fix-up. Most are sold for about ten dollars each. This series has one flaw: no single book covers everything you might need to know about one project. For instance, when we laid the terra-cotta tiles, I used three of their books. Another specialized book, a considerable investment that pays for itself the first time you service your own furnace, is *How to Buy, Repair and Maintain Home Systems and Appliances* by J. T. Adams, published by Arco Publishing ($29.95).

If you feel totally inept but have great hopes, start with a book that may not give all the details you'll eventually need but assumes you know nothing. Start by learning the proper way to use a hammer and progress to everything from electrical repairs to fixing windows that won't open to refinishing floors and furniture to repairing garden hoses and storm windows. There are dozens of books like this available.

A NOTE TO NOVICES

No matter how great your nerve and verve, there are projects you should not tackle alone yet. How many? Which ones? Only you can determine that, but here are a few clues:

If you rent, check with your landlord first. Better yet, let the landlord take care of it. Your rent should cover repairs necessary to keep the property up to snuff.

Don't monkey with anything still under warranty. First, the manufacturer is legally obligated to make it right. Second, there's no sense paying twice; manufacturers project repair risks into retail prices. Third, if you make the problem worse by messing with it, you may void your warranty.

Don't attempt major plumbing projects unless you have experienced help *beside* you (not over the telephone). Unclogging drains (sink, disposal, dishwasher, tub) and leaky faucets are common, easy-to-fix problems. (Remember to turn off the water source first!)

Don't do any house wiring unless you have a license. (I have a license, a homeowner's version. Of course, I had to study books for several evenings and take a test [not required by every jurisdiction]. Then, for safety's sake, I played apprentice to an electrician-friend for several days while he helped us wire our house.) Not only could you be fined for violating local building codes, but one little error could destroy your property—and you—or set the stage for a later catastrophe.

Nearly all of us, at one time or another, become so restless that we decide there's no place like home—that is, no place as dissatisfying as the home we're in. Decorators make their livelihood off this restlessness. I once met a woman who has her furniture reupholstered every two years. Some people merely move the furniture around. Others move to new houses. Some folks content themselves with a new coat of paint. Next time you get the itch for a new paint job, hold off the paint brush and roller for a few days. Meantime, dig out the scrub brush. Wash away the dinginess instead of covering it. See how you like the color that emerges before you paint over it. Your time's not wasted even if the color still displeases you; a good paint job requires a clean base.

Remember the allegory in this children's story, appropriate for all adults: Once upon a time there was an old lady who was dissatisfied with her little house, so she packed all her possessions and set off down the road. At the first corner she took a right-hand turn. A ways down that road she found a house that was "just right." As it was empty, she moved in and lived contentedly—for a few days. Then she became restless and moved on again. She took the first right turn and soon spotted a second "just right" house where she stayed for a short time. But again she became restless. She moved on a third time and a fourth. Finally, after a series of moves and right-hand turns, she reached the most "perfect" house of all. You guessed it! The perfect house was the one she'd left originally.

5

Stop
and
Swap

*A generous man will
prosper;
he who refreshes others
will himself be
refreshed.*

PROVERBS 11:25

Charge cards and chunky checking accounts aren't the only access to the "good life," as creative improvisers have recently rediscovered. They've learned to swap and share, using barter and cooperation instead of money to meet financial needs and to obtain a few of life's little extras.

Actually, co-ops are as old as neighborliness, barter as ancient as humanity's realization that total self-sufficiency is unpleasant, if not impossible. Barter was commonplace before shekels and shillings. Today, both barter and co-ops are reaching new heights of popularity as necessity "re-invents" substitutes for the shrinking dollar. Swapping and sharing are equally remunerative. And they're fun, polite ways to defy our money-minded and materialistic society.

Maybe you already barter without calling it by that name. Ever give a bachelor(ette) a couple of free dinners in exchange for an evening or two of baby-sitting? We do that all the time. My brother-in-law, Jim, does a few hours of diaper duty in return for a night or two away from frozen dinners or canned spaghetti. Along with the taste of homemade meatloaf, he gets a week's worth of vitamins from the greens at our dinner table. Ever mow your vacationing neighbors' lawns so they'll mow yours when you're away? That's barter. Ever split a bushel of peaches with someone? Go halves on a side of beef? That's a co-operative.

Baby-sitters, tools, food, clothes: that's just the beginning. Things you can't swap "free" you can get at reduced rates by banding together as a co-op. Sometimes the two, barter and co-op, are combined. Almost anything's possible.

BARTER

Barter is a labyrinth of possibilities. There's only one prerequisite. You must have something to trade, be it skill or merchandise or a combination of the two. If it's a skill, it should be, ideally, an activity you enjoy. If it's merchandise, it should be something you don't mind losing or something you enjoy producing. Remember the "You hang my cupboards and I'll bake your pies" swap in the last chapter? A distaste for baking or an inability to roll out a presentable crust would have complicated the barter. Perhaps the woman with the new cupboards could trade her empty pie pans and a few casserole dinners to a friend who can't cook but likes to bake and who would supply the cupboard hanger with the pie payments.

Barterers improvise as the situation demands, but they have a pretty good idea of the trade value of their talents, skills, interests, and goods. Polishing popular skills and accepting tradable goods for which they have no use or fondness but can easily swap later is the way barterers build "savings" accounts. A barterer's skills and accumulated surplus function as currency in the barter marketplace.

Currency, of course, is not of equal value. Its worth depends on need and desirability. People's needs for clothing, food, shelter, and health care are ever-present. Your services as a haircutter, baker, baby-sitter, tailor or jack/jill-of-all-trades will always be in demand. Plumbers and grease monkeys could live like royalty if they'd barter their skills. Some professionals have a head start: dentists, doctors, nurses, veterinarians, and lawyers can almost name their barter ticket. Those of us who "deal in paper" may have to look to our avocations for possible barter currency. But there's hope. If you're handy with a pencil you might swap a good newspaper story (of great value as advertising) for a month's worth of bread from your baker, a year's supply of trash bags from your neighborhood hardware store, several rolls of wallpaper from a decorator.

Antiques and artwork aren't always as easily traded as wheelbarrows or car tune-ups. But an artist who's all thumbs when it comes to fixing the front steps may find a handy but house-poor neighbor who could use a frescoed wall to cover up the fact that there's no furniture. (Would you believe that I even know of one art teacher who traded an original oil painting he had done for a piece of music composed just for him by a fellow music teacher.) Or an incapacitated elderly person with a house full of antique furnishings and a garage full of unused cars could work out deals with either the artist or the handy neighbor. The elderly person's car and excess furniture could be payment for an ever-changing, at-home art gallery, a weekly grocery trip, or the seasonal task of switching storm windows and screens.

The best barterers barter constantly. Not for them the theory that you can't afford it if you have to ask how much it costs. Barterers are not easily intimidated by price tags or repair bills. Such self-confidence comes with experience, but how does a shy, would-be barterer acquire experience?

As the saying goes, there's safety in numbers. Find other people who are interested in barter, and you're on your way to a barter club, a network which can take any of several forms. Some are so small, so low-key, that if you look around your community you may find one already thriving.

One way to interest prospective members in a barter network is by organizing a barter fair. In its simplest form, a barter fair is no more involved than a multi-household lawn sale. One example is the TAG (take and give) sale our church held last year. Everybody brought their surplus (or as much as they wanted to bring) and helped themselves to other people's bounty (as much as they could use). Some people brought very little but took home a lot, a fine system but highly unusual and probably unacceptable as a regular network practice.

A more farsighted introduction begins with a potluck supper, a true cooperative barter. You trade helpings of your casserole for a scoop of chocolate pudding, a few meatballs, a slice of homemade bread, etc. When everyone sits back, contentedly overfed, you explain the possibilities of extending the satisfaction they're experiencing at that moment, the result of barter, to goods and services they can swap indefinitely. Of course you've invited a broad mix of people, assembled every skill imaginable; there must be something for everyone. Besides the potential backbone of your network, you have the making of a great brainstorming session. Everybody likes to get in on the ground floor. It silences the malcontents who might say later, "Well, if I'd been there when they made the rules. . . ." Besides culling ideas for the intent and methods of your network, you'll realize what skills your network lacks and know what to look for when you recruit new members. But membership drives come later. First you have to organize, to establish the form and system of your network.

Every barter is an exchange, whether service for service, goods for goods, or service for goods. Every barter can be direct or indirect, thus the two common forms of networks—direct exchanges and indirect exchanges.

A direct exchange is the simplest, most informal

system. As the name implies, members exchange directly with each other, working out their own swaps and putting their own value, however uneven, on each swap. Because no bookkeeping is required, this kind of network can function relatively smoothly through a clearing house as minor as a "offer and needs" bulletin board convenient to all, but most networks of this type publish a catalog or directory, a sort of "yellow pages" which enumerate the network's resources: each member's skills, services, goods (to swap *and* to lend), extraneous details, ongoing needs, telephone numbers, and addresses. The usual disadvantages of direct exchange networks are the uneven value of the swaps and the limitation to one-to-one swaps.

An indirect exchange is slightly more complicated but offers the benefits of multiple (three, four, and five-way) trades and the opportunity to even out the values. Members of an indirect exchange might want a catalog, but their primary resource is a clearing house—perhaps nothing more complex than a file box of 3 x 5 cards. Each category or skill has its own card with appropriate members' names listed. Each member has an individual card, basically duplicating the catalog information but with the addition of a "balance sheet" on the flip side. The clearing house is, in effect, a "bank." Members take turns being "banker": arranging swaps, direct or multiple, and keeping track of "credits" and "debits." Membership doesn't preclude informal swaps of uneven value, of course, but in most indirect exchanges the value of each skill is predetermined. One variation of the credit/debit system makes life easier on the bookkeeper: individuals trade coupons or chits or tokens, much as they would trade dollar bills, perhaps establishing the value of each swap on a case-by-case basis. But barter currencies (coupons, etc.) should not be equated to dollars; they're illegal if they resemble too closely, even in function, an alternative currency.

Determining the value or parity of skills and services can be a sensitive issue. The simplest and most egalitarian method is to consider each member's time of equal value, however skilled or unskilled the labor. But what about those skills which require expensive equipment or years of costly training? A dentist, for example, has years of education and all his office rigging to pay for, as well as insurance and other expenses. The alternative is to establish parity or value according to modified market value. For instance, if baby-sitters charge a dollar per hour in your area, and the typical dentist's fee is twenty dollars per hour, you might equate one dental hour or "credit" to four baby-sitting hours or "credits," not twenty. But if the dentist is hard-pressed to find child care for a long-awaited night on the town and that evening happens to be an inconvenient one for the baby-sitter, who agrees to help anyway, a one-to-one swap is fair.

Some services require no skills as such but are worthy swaps and should be noted under "extraneous" in the catalog or on the member's clearing house card. For example, someone who works next to a post office can accumulate a cache of credits (or casual IOUs, if it's a direct exchange network) during the Christmas season by standing in line a few times to mail everybody's packages and cards. Some swaps may be for exactly the same service. Ever hear of quilting bees? Barn raisings? If you've ever baled hay or fenced in a pasture, you know the value of teamwork. Team effort sometimes makes the difference between winning the race against that threatening thundercloud and losing the last wagonload of hay to a drenching downpour. Anyone who has knocked in a few fence posts appreciates the value of taking turns.

Take advantage of the lessons already learned by a successfully functioning barter network which has already worked out the snarls your local group anticipates or may already be experiencing. The Community Skills Exchange of Olympia, Washington, offers a packet (for $6.00) which, they say, includes everything you need to set up your own "skills bank," an exchange featuring services rather than goods. As well as sample forms and ledger sheets and other record-keeping aids, the packet relates the group's history, including their problems and solutions. Write to Community Skills Exchange, 921 North Rogers Street, Olympia, Washington 98502.

Barter Clubs

Big-time barter clubs exemplify "too much of a good thing," at least for the average person who barters for the necessities or a few extras. Big barter clubs are for-profit national organizations, sometimes with local franchises. They require high, and sometimes annual, membership fees. Certain clubs require a percentage fee from every swap, and members are not allowed to swap with each other outside the club's system. However, barter clubs serve a necessary function for a limited percentage of the population. If you produce something which has a limited market locally, a barter club may be a good idea. For instance, if you breed AKC wolfhounds, your hometown or county may be able to absorb only so many; a barter club increases your market.

Joining a big, expensive, nationwide club isn't the only way to extend your barter avenues past your own city limits. Several magazines and newspapers have swap columns. Granddaddy to all of them may be the "Original Yankee Swopper's Column." Nearly forty years old, *Yankee* magazine's swop (sic) column publishes (free) several dozen swaps each month. Swaps are selected randomly from the hundreds they receive. If your swap isn't published within six months or so of the time you send it in, they advise that you reenter it. Send your swap to *Yankee,* Dublin, New Hampshire 03444. You might first check out an issue to see what typical "swops" look like. Many are for land or real estate. A *Yankee* subscription is fourteen dollars, but you need not be a subscriber to use the column.

Vacation Clubs

Assuming you can afford transportation, you can barter for temporary housing in almost any corner of the earth. How? You swap houses.

I have a friend in Copenhagen who's been begging me for years to swap houses for a summer. Maybe we will, sometime. I have another friend who already swaps on a regular basis. She's a New Yorker, born and bred, who now finds herself on a remote farm in rural Virginia. Occasionally the chirping birds and sweet fresh air become too much for her to bear, so she and her husband swap houses with city friends in Washington, D.C.

You can, of course, swap houses with a member of your local club, but unless someone has a vacation retreat available the swap may not get you much further than your own backyard. Vacation clubs are an exception to the general rule about the worthlessness of huge barter clubs. By using their services, you can retreat to virtually anyplace you can afford to go, your housing free if you have a house or apartment to offer in exchange. It helps if you live in a desirable location, of course: in or near a popular city, deep in the woods, beside a lake or river, near an ocean, high on a mountain, on a farm. Some small towns are desirable, too. The rapid growth of these clubs speaks well for their popularity. Some clubs publish only one listing annually; others have small circulation or a high listing fee. Most offer a handbook detailing what's expected of house-swappers. Before you sign on, ask the quantity of listings as well as the circulation, how many listings your fee entitles you to, and how often the listings are published. Here are addresses for these clubs:

Vacation Exchange Club
350 Broadway
New York, NY 10013

Holiday Exchanges
Box 878
Belen, NM 87002

Inquiline, Inc.
35 Adams Street
Bedford Hills, NY 10507

DON'T FORGET UNCLE SAM

The results of your barter aren't always pure gravy. The Internal Revenue Service wants its cut. They're primarily concerned about the number of high-value trades, particularly those which amount to illegal tax shelters for business. Of less concern are friendly swaps, one neighbor doing a favor for another. Obviously, if the favors are for people you wouldn't know if it weren't for your barter network, the line of distinction is a fine one to be carefully considered. But keep in mind that there's nothing wrong with having a wide circle of friends.

The IRS expects individuals to report the fair market value of goods and services received through barter as income on their tax returns. How do you establish fair market value for such services as standing in line at the post office? The IRS might make its estimate according to what was given in exchange for that time in line. They say, "If you agree ahead of time to the value of services, that value will be accepted as fair market value unless shown otherwise" (*Highlights of 1979 Tax Changes*, IRS Publication # 553). Business people can deduct certain swaps as business expenses. For example, dental work swapped for a redecorated office qualifies; dental work swapped for a redecorated living room does not. (The decorator can deduct her swap as a medical expense.)

The tax implications of barter are enumerated and well-described in two books any barter organizer ought to read, although the two books use slightly differing nomenclature for types of barter. *What'll You Take for It? Back to Barter,* by Annie Proulx, is particularly helpful to rural barterers. Order it ($5.95) from Garden Way Publishing, Charlotte, Vermont 05445. You may also find a Pocket Books version in a local bookstore. *The Barter Network Handbook: Building Community Through Organized Barter,* by David Tobin and Henry Ware, is full of methods and organizational tips. Tobin is the bartering community's "man in Washington"; he has his finger on the pulse of bartering efforts nationwide, and his book reflects his experience. This brand-new book is available from Volunteer Readership, P.O. Box 1807, Boulder, Colorado 80306. ($5.95 plus $2.25 postage and handling).

COOPERATIVES

Some co-operatives might be just as correctly called barter groups. Baby-sitting co-ops and car pools are two common examples. But most cooperatives function as buying clubs, allowing members to take advantage of group rates and bulk discounts. Three examples are housing co-ops, food co-ops, and legal co-ops.

Housing Co-ops

Housing co-ops, like all cooperatives, are owned by their customers. A housing co-op is formalized neighborliness which offers such luxuries as pool and tennis courts—as well as your basic roof-over-the-head—individuals couldn't otherwise afford. Many types of housing co-ops exist, all beyond the scope of this book. For information about housing co-ops, write to The National Consumer Cooperative Bank, 2001 S Street NW, Washington, D.C. 20009. For information on starting a housing co-op contact The National Association of Housing Cooperatives, 1012 14th Street NW, Washington, D.C. 20005.

Food Co-ops

The forms a food co-op can take are nearly as varied as the total number of such co-ops. Some limit themselves to one type of food, fresh produce being a popular example. Some restrict membership to a handful of neighbors. But the possibilities are almost infinite. One food co-op, the Puget Consumers Cooperative in Seattle, grew from fifteen households (who in 1960 decided to buy their vegetables and fruit together at wholesale prices) to over fifteen thousand (who today own two supermarkets with five million dollars in annual sales).

Some people erroneously assume that co-ops require each member to commit several hours of grueling labor each week. Good co-ops do not, once they've been successfully launched. As a matter of fact, the bigger the co-op, the greater the return for the least individual effort. Even so, you should start small, assembling members with similar food preferences. Not that everybody must like asparagus or whatever, but every household must like the *type* of food—produce, dairy products, meat—you collectively agree to cut your teeth on. A half-dozen or so households is a large enough membership to allow the co-op to take advantage of bulk discounts, purchase a variety, and use up the food before it spoils.

A five-household produce co-op in our town works like this: Each Tuesday morning one member goes, at crack of dawn (before daylight in winter months), to the wholesale produce market ten miles away. The member carries cash to purchase the group's weekly consumption: three bushels of fruit and three of vegetables. Keeping in mind the possibility of. leftovers from last week's purchases, the member finds six bushels worth of food she/he 1) knows will please the palates of the other members and 2) are bargains. Usually she/he brings home at least eight or nine kinds of food (as half-bushels and odd-sized cartons extend the variety). By the end of the day the member has divvied up each food into five equal piles and delivered it to members' homes along with an after-the-fact shopping list and the bill—paid on the spot or within a few days. When one member is on vacation, the bounty is decreased by a half-bushel. If it unexpectedly turns out that one household detests peas or artichokes or whatever, the shopper usually trades a share of her own pile for the food in question, the policy being that if the shopper likes it enough to buy it, her family won't mind a double dose. This co-op is about as simple as one can be.

The quantity of food a co-op purchases depends on members' needs and whether they consider the co-op a supplement or a substitute for regular shopping. Since the intent of the venture is not to complicate life but to simplify it, the system should be designed to allow members to order enough variety and quantity that they can detour around that particular grocery aisle on their regular shopping expedition. The co-op illustrated assumes any one member always has enough cash in hand to cover a large order. For some co-ops this might be a problem.

The solution is "seed money." New members put into a kitty an amount roughly equal to one week's purchase (estimated through the group's practice visit to the wholesale market). The first shopper uses the cash kitty; then, when reimbursed, passes it on to the next shopper. A kitty should always have about 20 percent more in it than the shopper expects to use. Prices invariably increase despite seasonal drops. When a member leaves the co-op, they take their share of the kitty.

Wholesale produce markets are located anywhere there's an abundance of grocery stores. Some charge an entrance fee of a few dollars. All have various stalls which either specialize or sell a little bit of everything. Shop around for bargains and quality. At some markets you collect tickets or vouchers, then pay at a central desk. At other markets you pay the vendor directly. Some markets have loading docks where buyers present loaders with vouchers. (Always check your merchandise before it's loaded; a random mushy orange is not cause for return, but several are. You might even be mistakenly given another buyer's order.) At other places buyers must fend for themselves. Remember that vendors operate on a first-come, first-served basis: the best stuff goes early. Most markets deal only in cash, and some expect buyers to provide their own crates (reusable).

Wholesale markets aren't the only way to buy fresh produce. Co-ops can buy directly from farmers, sometimes getting as much variety with little extra effort. Members benefit by getting the freshest of fresh, and the small farmer, often ignored by big-time commercial buyers, benefits from co-op business. Farmers may take orders by telephone and make deliveries, or they may require buyers to come to the farm. Remember that farmers usually can't spare the expense of baskets and crates. You may have to put down a deposit or provide your own. The better the relation a co-op establishes with the farmer, the more expansive the opportunities. For instance, a produce farmer who learns to trust your co-op may "put you onto" the dairy farmer down the road whose cows are in a very generous mood. They're giving more cream than the dairy farmer knows what to do with. Homemade ice cream, any-one? Another of the farmer's neighbors may be planning to turn his porkers into bacon and chops and could use your one-time business. Here's where a kitty and the co-op's open attitude comes in.

Dairy products consume a large chunk of most families' food budgets. Joining a co-op with dairy farmer connections makes good sense. Dairy whole-sale distributors are a good idea if everybody in the co-op likes butter and cream and yogurt or just drinks gallons of milk weekly. The money you save on discounted milk may pay for the cream for your strawberries. When you investigate dairy distributors, you'll need to determine what they deal in, the unit amounts and bulk-sale discounts, as well as their delivery policies. Here are some specific questions:

Does milk come in both gallon and half-gallon sizes? If so, what's the price difference? What's the price of cardboard cartons compared to plastic?

If they handle cheese, in what sizes and what kinds? Domestic and imported? If so, can they describe where the cheese is from? (Different locales produce similarly named cheese of quite different flavor.)

What size are butter or margarine blocks? Are they wrapped in paper or boxed? Which is cheaper?

Do they offer cottage cheese? What curd? What size are the containers and how many per carton?

How many of what size (and flavor) of yogurt come per carton? Can they mix flavors in a carton?

Will they deliver to a private residence for free? If so, how large must the order be? If not, where and when can you make connections?

Is the truck refrigerated?

Is a deposit required for crates?

Another big slice of the food budget pays for baked goods, for which co-ops can go to three sources: huge, regional wholesale operations which supply supermarkets with breads and rolls; regional representatives of the specialty chains (e.g., English muffins or dessert rolls); and local bakeries. Besides determining what is available, when and where, the co-op needs to know the discounts available per unit order: Are two dozen loaves (or two dozen packages of English muffins) cheaper per loaf than one dozen?

By the time a co-op has expanded to include dairy products, bread, perhaps even staples such as peanut butter and rice, it's probably beyond the scope of a Tuesday (or Monday or whenever) kitchen-counter task. Farmers will need a central number; they can't be expected to keep track of whose responsibility falls on what particular week. The co-op also needs a mailing address and a bank account for safekeeping of the considerable amount of cash flow. The simple kitty system won't be adequate. In short, the co-op now requires a team effort each week. Nobody wants the obligation of shopping for *everything* for six or eight or twelve or two dozen households, even if their turn comes up only once in a blue moon. And no six (or two dozen) families will have such identical shopping lists. This is the point where short-sighted co-ops decide the project is too much of a headache and chuck the whole thing.

But for those farsighted souls in this world, the sky's the limit. They now realize they have reached the point where just ahead, with a little rearrangement of their *modus operandi*, lies even *greater* return for considerably *less* individual effort. This is when they move the kitchen-counter brigade to someone's back porch or garage, when a member with bookkeeping skills is relieved from shopping responsibilities but designs an order-and-payment system, when shopping chores are divvied up (perhaps one person permanently handling baked goods, another dairy products, while other members take turns shopping for produce). Whatever's equitable and whatever's necessary to keep the prices low and labor light, that's the direction the burgeoning co-op takes. By this time there's likely to be a waiting list of eager joiners and a grapevine connection to other co-ops. There's a whole national network of possibilities!

Meantime, though, what you need for starters is

a set of used baby scales (for weighing produce and grains), a few eager neighbors and friends, and more information. Write to the Cooperative League of the U.S.A. (1828 L St. NW, Suite 1100, Washington, D.C. 20036) which can set you on the right track.

Legal Co-ops

Still relatively rare outside labor unions and the like, legal co-ops are an idea worth considering for organizations whose members need a lawyer occasionally. And who doesn't? There is no typical legal co-op, more commonly known as "plan." The idea behind them is to make legal services available to people who should use them but for economic reasons do not. The lawyers, of course, benefit by getting business they might not have otherwise. Also, the lawyer usually gets a retainer fee for agreeing to give legal help at reduced rates. Sometimes the help is advice on *pro se* (do it yourself) law.

Before your group approaches an attorney to set up such a system, a bit of reading is in order. Write to the National Resource Center for Consumers of Legal Services, 1302 18th St. NW, Washington, D.C. 20036. Ask for general information and, specifically, the publications list which makes available collected articles on legal clinics, assessing needs, selecting a lawyer, various plans already functioning, and organizing a plan.

MEMORIAL SOCIETIES

Death may seem an odd expense to cooperate on, hardly a consumer good, but at second glance the reasons are perfectly clear. The average funeral, including burial, costs almost three thousand dollars. A figure twice that high is not uncommon. Who pays? The deceased's loved ones pick up the tab, frequently digging deep into the insurance resources intended for living—not burial—expenses. A lifetime membership in a memorial society costs no more than twenty-five dollars (more often half that amount) and reduces funeral expenses to an average below one thousand dollars. As well as saving two thousand dollars by spending twenty-five, members save on life insurance; their own funeral expenses are one thing they don't need to worry about.

Memorial societies also offer an opportunity to plan a funeral that is economically appropriate for your individual circumstances, perhaps emphasizing spiritual rather than material values. The first memorial society, in fact, was organized by a small church group in Seattle in 1939. Most societies today are nonsectarian and nonprofit and were organized by either church groups or consumer cooperatives. Volunteers staff the two hundred societies (a million members) nationwide.

You can contact a local society or write to the Continental Association of Funeral and Memorial Societies, Suite 1100, 1828 L St. NW, Washington, D.C. 20036. CAFMS responds to general inquiries with a small brochure, *Last Rights*, and a directory. Both are free. If you need advice on organizing a society or preplanning without a society, send $2.50 (plus 50¢ postage) and request *A Manual of Death Education and Simple Burial*, which also includes information on anatomical gifts.

6

Ribeye on a Soybean Budget

*Do not eat the food of a
stingy man,
do not crave his
delicacies;
for he is the kind of man
who is always thinking
about the cost.*

PROVERBS 23:6, 7

I love huge, extravagant feasts. I derive more pleasure from their planning and preparation than I do in the actual eating. Some people like to tuck in early for a long, relaxing evening with a novel or a TV movie; I prefer to cuddle up with several back issues of *Bon Appétit*, a couple of cookbooks, three or four dozen scraps of paper to serve as bookmarks, and several hours in which to dream up my next dinner party.

But few tasks do I detest more than the preparing of everyday suppers.

It was easy when I went to the office every day. Jack and I alternated monthly KP. When he cooked, I cleaned up. And vice versa. Whenever either of us felt disinclined to our respective duties, we went out. That meant we ate out at least once, usually twice, a week.

These little kitchen intermissions were not spent at posh places, by any means. Usually they meant the Ranch House, a local eatery not quite fast food, not quite night out, where you can get a chicken dinner including salad and baked potato for barely four dollars. Add dessert and coffee—as many refills as you want—plus tip, and one person's tab is still under six dollars. Better yet, children's menus (hot dogs, grilled cheese, and the like) are a dollar apiece. With each child's meal you get a coupon; when you collect six coupons the child's meal is on the house. Not bad, even if most of the child's nutrition is in the glass of milk. But do this half a dozen times a month and you've spent what amounts to a nice cartful of groceries.

Obviously, when we cut our income in half, the

pattern had to change. We could not continue to entertain the way we liked *and* eat out as the mood struck us *and* keep any kind of decent food around for everyday fare.

I had to shift perspective. A mediocre, six-dollar chicken dinner once a week could be traded in on a nine-dollar dinner at a better place every other week. We'd still be ahead. That was the first step. Second was trading in that nine-dollar dinner for two weekly steak dinners at home. Third, we traded the two steak dinners for two chicken and one steak. Last, we settled on a less expensive cut of steak so that we now have two chicken and two steak.

We now belong to two groups, seemingly dichotomous, of the American grocery-buying public: those who have chicken at least twice weekly and those who have steak at least twice weekly. Granted, ours are neither ten-ounce servings nor prime rib. We usually divvy up one large chuck. Trimmed and broiled, slightly rare, it is delicious.

I buy our steak from an old-time butcher who takes pride in his work. I pay a few pennies more per pound but there's little waste, unlike the assembly-line packaged meat from the supermarkets. Furthermore, now that I'm a regular, my butcher points me to that day's best buys; he tells me what's in the back room awaiting the chopping block, which he'll put into immediate use at my request. His merits don't end there. *Before* the meat goes on the scale, he trims off the fat that in most places would be neatly tucked out of place beneath the cellophane. We eat better meat and as much—for less money—than almost anyone I know.

Another bargain source I discovered is the bakery. The price of bakery bread is comparable to the house brand at the supermarket nearby. And the quality at least equals the high-priced brands I used to buy at that grocery. Not all bakeries offer such good value, but once you find one, you're all set.

A few of my new habits are old hat to many shoppers. Coupon clipping, for instance. Unfortunately, the majority of coupons offered are for high-caloried, low-nutrition garbage. A package of bologna is money wasted, in my opinion, no matter how great the price reduction. On the other hand, twenty cents off the regular price of my family's favorite peanut butter means I get that one instead of the store brand. Coupons for fifty cents or a dollar have always caught my eye, but I couldn't be bothered with the ten or fifteen-cent variety. Their sum total of a dollar or two or, occasionally, three, was not worth the embarrassment of emptying the contents of my purse onto the checkout counter, looking for the right coupon, which might not be there anyway because I could never remember whether I had saved that coupon for "x" brand or merely intended to or had used it last shopping trip or given it away. Or was it "y" brand I was thinking of? All this for an expired coupon! No wonder coupon clippers are the butt of many jokes! Now I spend two minutes maximum scanning the Thursday and Sunday food sections of my newspaper and save about four dollars each month; I do a one-minute review of the coupon inventory *before* I enter the store. The fifty dollars or so this saves us each year I consider a year's worth of free coffee or laundry detergent or yogurt. (No, I do not yet make our yogurt. But I will, I will.)

We save another four or five dollars per month by taking advantage of certain nearby stores' occasional "triple coupon" sales; for each manufacturer's coupon I take in, that store triples the redemption up to a dollar. Usually these sales are offered by stores I shun because of their typically high prices; the two or three genuine bargains they might offer in a usual week would not be worth the trouble of a special trip. However, during triple coupon week I take advantage of those items as well as the triple coupon offer. I put nothing in my shopping bag unless it represents a saving of at least 30 percent under that store's normal price, at least 20 percent under what I'd expect to pay.

Another new habit is my odyssey, every four to six weeks, to a food warehouse. Some people call these "discount groceries." More frequent junkets are not worth the fuel it takes to get there because not everything there beats the weekly specials I find at groceries closer to home. But I consistently find their chicken two-thirds the price at closer stores, so I buy at least ten meals worth. When unexpected company comes, there's always plenty. Also for the freezer are several dollars worth of vegetables bearing unfamiliar brand names. They don't taste like fresh homegrown, but neither does anything else bought out of season, fresh or not. For this reason I also tote home a cupboardful of canned goods. They're fine in soups and stews. Perishables, unfortunately, are the best deal warehouses offer. For this reason alone it would be nice to have one closer. They consistently undersell everybody else. When other places sell bananas for 39¢ a pound, I can get them there three pounds for $1. When other places drop them to three pounds for $1, the warehouse has them marked 28¢ per pound. So it goes, up and down that entire aisle of fresh produce. We feast on fresh foods for at least a week. Whatever's showing its age by then, I camouflage by throwing into a soup or stew. The bananas with blackening skins I throw into the freezer to use in custards or baking; the insides stay fine. This single, bag-your-own, inconvenient, out-of-the-way trip to the warehouse saves us $10 to $15 per month. With its help we've cut our grocery tab, including light bulbs and laundry soaps and the rest of it, to an average of about $35 per week for four people. That's no headline maker, to be sure, but neither is it macaroni and cheese.

Speaking of cheese, we consume about two pounds of the good stuff—real stuff—each week. One of the greatest supermarket ripoffs is that over-processed rubber called cheese product. Another, lesser, monstrosity is cheese already sliced or grated. Blindfolded, put some of these to a taste test, comparing the store-bought processed or grated or sliced versions with a quality version of that same cheese. Can you match them? Parmesan, especially, becomes almost unrecognizable. So does its price. Parmesan loses much of its flavor when grated far ahead of the time it is served; a chunk of the real thing from the deli tastes infinitely better, lasts (ungrated) for months in the refrigerator, and costs far less than the powdery, packaged stuff sold by the ounce.

Sometimes you don't need to shop a deli to get deli-quality products. The cheddar cheese we put away pound after pound is an example. On our semi-annual trips to visit family in western New York, we make it a point to visit Cuba Cheese, where we purchase one or two ten-pound blocks which we cut into two-to-three-pound chunks when we get home. Some chunks we freeze; the rest we distribute to friends who have placed "orders." (If you visit Cuba Cheese—or any "food factory"—inquire about lower-priced irregulars [in shape only] stored in the back room.) I had to search several stores in our local community before I found one that regularly stocks a satisfactory substitute. We like our cheddar white (no orange coloring) and very sharp. The cheddar I found was not as sharp as our family likes, but for $2.79 per pound as opposed to the deli's $4.00 plus, we adjusted to the milder flavor. Still, I kept checking the cheese bins of every grocery I happened to visit. Finally, on a visit to the A&P (generally too expensive for the bulk of our shopping but worth a stop for their coffee beans), I found a cheddar on a par with the deli version. The price was only ten cents more per pound than the version we'd made suffice. Now, when I make my monthly stop for A&P coffee beans, I pick up $15 to $20 worth of cheddar. Outrageous price, you say, when a "two-pound loaf of the other stuff" costs just slightly more than $3? Check out what the nutritionists have to say about an ounce for ounce, penny for penny comparison. I'll stick with the natural, additive-free—and delicious—variety.

"All these monthly 'stops'!" you exclaim. "Do I spend my days racing from store to store, obsessed with nickels and dimes and quality?" Hardly. I hate any kind of grocery shopping, and, as I've already stated, detest wasting time on everyday suppers. Why else would I buy twenty dollars worth of cheese on a single shopping trip? I time my coffee-and-cheese runs to the A&P to coincide with their triple coupon sales. My dreaded monthly foray to the discount warehouse cuts the rest of my shopping to the one or two-bag type, a nuisance I can live with. This kind of shopping relieves me of tedious menu planning because I use what's on hand—there's usually plenty.

A time or two each month, this means a huge pot of soup or stew. I scrounge through the vegetable bins, dragging out everything withered. From the freezer I pull the plastic bag of assorted, leftover bones and vegetables that have accumulated since the last pottage. Everything goes into the biggest pot we own, is covered with water and plenty of herbs, then left untended for hours. Any deficiency I discover later, I compensate for with a can or two of vegetables—fresh ones if it's summer. Most of this concoction I freeze in whatever ex-mayo or peanut butter jars are handy, and we have ready four or five "free" meals for the labor of just one. Add some good bread and cheese, and dinner's served. That kind of easy cooking keeps me from the Ranch House. It also cuts down on the utility bill.

Most other evenings I rely on two-pan suppers, a basic list of two dozen or so family favorites that we "mix and match" but which dirty no more than two, possibly three, pans. Admittedly, a pan sometimes serves a dual purpose; broccoli is kept covered and warm in its serving dish while the pan is reused for cheese sauce. Meantime, the rice is kept warm while I reuse *that* pan to stir-fry diced meat and vegetables. This system, beloved by the dishwasher (usually my husband), also contributes to keeping the Ranch House temptation under control.

That basic list of two dozen recipes does not mean our meals are monotonous; the list varies by season. Our table shows more variety than some of those I am familiar with, where a child could grow up assuming that uniform four-inch stalks are natural to asparagus and that it grows year-round; they see only the canned and frozen versions of almost every vegetable and fruit they eat, served without regard to season. Food served in its natural season tastes better—not just because we appreciate the lower cost of it fresh, but because it also has more flavor. Guests at *our* table are served asparagus only during a few short weeks in spring. Home gardeners with freezers or storage cellars can, of course, modify this rule, but for the majority of us there should be few exceptions. (Our family's one exception is Christmas morning brunch when we serve strawberries in fruit compote.)

Tomatoes may be the most abused food. In February, to eat tomatoes any other way than out of a can, is tasteless and expensive. Better to enjoy them in spaghetti sauce where the flavor is recognizable. Two or three times during the peak of tomato season I stop in at a fresh produce market, timing my visit to coincide with the hour they clean out bins, discarding the unmarketable (which would pass for first class in February). First, I load my cart with produce I need anyway; then I head straight to the manager or manager's assistant (clerks and stockboys hesitate to make decisions, I've found) and ask what their plans are for the discards. Usually I can walk away with a half bushel or so of barely bruised tomatoes for fifty cents. Another quarter or two gets me a few pounds each of onions and peppers in similar, second-rate, condition. Sometimes, if I mention it, they throw in some wilting parsley. For a dollar or two total (I also buy the choicest bunch of basil) I have myself the makings of enough tomato sauce for at least six meals. Some of it we consume immediately. Most of it I freeze in eighteen-ounce jars to pull out and enjoy in bitter winter when warm, basil-tomato-pepper days of August seem nothing but a dream. Even diluted by a can of tomato juice, this recaptures for us the essence of those summer flavors. Admittedly, each batch of sauce involves an hour of skinning tomatoes and chopping onions and peppers. But the reward we enjoy each time we open a jar compensates for the energy expended many months earlier.

Plus it's nice to know the freezer holds several ready-made entrees at about five cents a serving.

And get this—you don't have to have a super-sized freezer in the basement or garage. Ours is just the space on top of our refrigerator. (Winters, we don't keep it full of ice cream.) By those cold months when I fill it with soups and stews and frozen vegetables, the tomato sauce is on the wane. Similarly, there's less chicken when the thermometer's at 90°F and appetites are listless. Those are the days for a freezer of ice cream and a refrigerator full of watermelon.

Every season has its offerings. Corn-on-the-cob and early, tart apples come just in time to ease the loss of tomatoes-and-cucumbers, peaches-and-blueberries. Pumpkins are a three-month-long bonanza. Then come cranberries and time to remember the ever humble, but faithful, cabbage. Oranges and grapefruit manage to linger until the wait for early peas and strawberries seems tolerable. And thus another annual cycle. The ubiquitous carrot pulls us through the entire year. I mention these particular foods because they're plentiful and cheap and remain family favorites despite the fact that we eat them several times weekly in their respective seasons. By the end of each one's "season" we've had enough to satisfy us until the next year. The old reliables, you might say. Most require no "recipe"; how does one botch peaches and blueberries? Most can be fixed in endless numbers of ways, needing only a new "twist" to keep them from becoming monotonous.

Take the pumpkin, for instance. Bless it. Maybe it's the appeal of Halloween, but my daughter loves the pumpkin with almost as much fervor as she dislikes most other squash. A wonderful accommodation on her part, as the pumpkin is as multifarious in its roles as any food can be. It can star in anything from soup to dessert. It is incredibly cheap if you don't buy it by the pound. Come early September, we begin to scan farmers' stands and likely looking rural places for a glimpse of telltale orange—the first of our stock which we replenish a couple of times as the season wears on. Usually, for a couple of dollars, we carry home a trunkful of medium-sized orange beauties and a giant for JC's jack-o'-lantern fantasies. Pumpkins keep well for several weeks in a cool dark place, but once they're cooked they spoil within a week or so. That's why we get the small-to-medium size: that, and my favorite pumpkin recipe—stuffed pumpkin. I learned it from Sharon Osgood of western New York, where pumpkins are as plentiful as autumn leaves. This is a sensational buffet dish (surround it with beautiful autumn leaves). Novelty that it is, it's almost equally good as a dinner entree for company. For a dinner table, the pumpkin should be on the small side. My apologies that this recipe is not more formal in appearance; you'll understand why when you read it.

Stuffed Pumpkin

First, wash the pumpkin and remove the top quarter or third in one piece, leaving the stem on (for appearance). Remove all the stringy insides and the seeds (saving the seeds to be rinsed and roasted for a later treat). Replace the top on the pumpkin and set it in a baking dish which you place in a 250°F oven, while you prepare the stuffing. Here's what makes your pumpkin unique; the stuffing varies according to your own preferences. Personally, the spicier it is the better we like it; maybe that's because "hot and spicy" gleans the most compliments. "Spicy" requires more sausage than a blander version, roughly two pounds of hot, country-style sausage for a pumpkin eight to twelve inches in diameter. Should you prefer a less spicy version, substitute hamburg for some of the sausage. Or mix in rice or croutons. Remember that pumpkin meat, like all squash, is bland; when scooped out with the filling it dilutes the spice considerably. For this reason you may want to serve the spicier version at dinner (with cornbread, perhaps?) and save the milder version as a buffet item to be dished up by crackers or breadsticks. Crackers tend to dig out considerably more filling than pumpkin and can leave the mouth burning. But if you're serving lots of cider. . . .

Back to the recipe. Brown the meat, adding oregano, salt, pepper. I use about two teaspoons of oregano, one-quarter teaspoon of pepper (preferably red), and no salt. Add one chopped onion and brown. If you have green or red peppers or leftover vegetables going to waste in your refrigerator, add them too. Drain off most of the grease, add rice or croutons, and set the filling aside until the pumpkin seems *slightly* cooked on the inside (approximately one hour from the time you put it into the oven). Be careful when you remove the top; it's becoming fragile. Put the filling into the pumpkin, replace the top, return to the oven, and forget about it for another hour or so. When it's done the pumpkin meat will be tender (almost soggy) and the filling hot to the touch. If you keep the top on, the whole thing will stay hot for several hours. Indeed, the bottom part will continue to "cook." (Great for taking to a potluck or autumn picnic. Just move it gently.)

Some recipes I've seen but never tried suggest parboiling the pumpkin just until tender, stuffing it, then baking it only half an hour or so. Another option I've never tried is a topping of grated cheese, probably cheddar, colby, or muenster.

Pumpkin soup is a cheap and novel way to begin an autumn or winter dinner party. Follow the soup with roast chicken or stir-fried pork; both are inexpensive. The taste of the first soup recipe is quite unusual (make your servings very small and use leftovers in a custard) and very sophisticated—somewhat ironic considering its "primitive" origins. I adapted it from a recipe in *Native Harvests, Recipes and Botanicals of the American Indian*. Do not expect similar results from English walnuts! Note the "precise" measurements!

Black Walnut and Pumpkin Soup

1 small pumpkin, cooked* (app. 2–3 cups)
1 cup black walnuts, chopped
maple syrup, to taste (app. ½ cup pure or artificial)
3–4 cups water
optional: roasted pumpkin seeds as garnish

*To cook a pumpkin, roast it in a 350°F oven or on the stove, in water, until the skin wrinkles and is easily pierced. The seeds and stringy part can be removed either before or after cooking.

Spoon the pumpkin meat into a saucepan and mash it with the syrup and ⅔ cup of black walnuts, adding enough water to liquefy to the desired consistency. Mix well and simmer, covered, for 3–5 minutes. Serve, garnished with roasted pumpkin seeds and/or a spoonful of chopped nuts.

(serves 6–8)

Everyday Pumpkin Soup

3 cups cooked pumpkin
1 quart chicken stock or ½ quart stock plus
 ½ quart tomato juice
1 bunch green onions
2 cups milk
ripe or canned tomato for garnish (optional)

Combine the pumpkin and chicken stock and bring to a boil. Reduce heat and simmer while you chop the onions. Add the white parts to the pumpkin/chicken and cook until tender. (Optional: run the mixture through a sieve or blender). Serve each bowlful topped with chopped green onion tops and a slice of tomato (ripe or canned).

There are endless dessert-type uses for pumpkins: cookies, custards, cakes, and, of course, pumpkin pie. I found this recipe in *Blair & Ketchum's Country Journal,* a wonderful magazine to which everyone should be given a Christmas gift subscription.

Pumpkin Pudding

¼ cup butter or margarine
½ cup maple syrup (pure is better, but artificial will suffice)

½ teaspoon cinnamon (or more, to taste)
½ teaspoon ground mace
3 eggs
1 cup puréed pumpkin (cooked as in the recipes above)
2 tablespoons rum flavoring
whipping cream (optional)

Preheat oven to 350°F. Cream butter and maple syrup together. Add spices. Beat in eggs and pumpkin, blending well. Stir in rum. Turn into buttered 1½ quart baking dish. Bake for 30 to 40 minutes until puffed and firm. Serve warm with rum-flavored whipped cream (optional). Serves 6 delicate appetites or the 4 hearty ones in our family.

One last pumpkin recipe I include because you're unlikely to come across it anywhere else. A batch of these fritters and lots of cider is a great way to provide a good, fun and unusual snack food for a crowd. Or serve them as an hors d'oeuvre or at a brunch or for Sunday night supper or with a meat course. Serve them plain or dusted with powdered sugar. The charming little book where I found the recipe, *The New England Butt'ry Shelf Almanac*, suggests serving them with maple syrup for breakfast or as a dessert. I never have; even my insatiable sweet tooth knows when enough is enough.

Pumpkin Fritters

2 cups cooked pumpkin
2 eggs beaten light
pinch of salt
½ teaspoon (or more) cinnamon
¼ teaspoon each nutmeg and ground cloves
½ cup milk

1 cup flour
2 teaspoons baking powder
2 tablespoons sugar

Mix ingredients together and drop by rounded teaspoonfuls into deep fat, heated to 375°F. Cook until browned, turn and brown on other side. Drain on paper towels. (Optional: dust with powdered sugar.) Makes a good-sized basketful.

Do I rave about pumpkin? Yes, and justly so. It's cheap, nourishing, and tasty. Yet it has not been "discovered"; more correctly, it has been forgotten. But if the zucchini can reach those giddy heights of popularity it seems to have reached, imagine the pumpkin's potential!

Another underrated vegetable is the cabbage. Because I'm not much on coleslaw, this bargain was virtually ignored by me until a woman (one who could have dined daily on caviar) treated me to her dish of preference. Like myself, this woman has better things to do with her day than spend it preparing supper. Also like myself, she has a weakness for butter. Sound familiar? Here's her recipe, now our family's all-time favorite vegetable. Nothing takes less time, except perhaps ripping open a bag of frozen peas.

Jo's Cabbage

Chop a small head of cabbage into strips ½ to 1 inch wide. Dump them into a pan in which you've melted about half a stick of margarine or butter. Cover and let steam/simmer in its own moisture for about 15 minutes. Salt and pepper to your taste (sometimes I throw in a few dill or poppy seeds) and serve immediately. Serves 4 to 6.

The secret to Jo's Cabbage is its lack of water. Nothing kills cabbage's naturally mild, sweet taste faster. This spells problems if you want to stuff a cabbage because, of course, the leaves must be removed through steaming or some other form of water cooking. Who wants to stuff a cabbage, anyway? It's not impressive company fare, even if the price is right, and it's too much trouble for everyday.

Which leads us to Cabbage Skillet Dinner, an honest-to-goodness, one-pan supper. I have little use for those conglomerations touted as one-dish dinners that dirty three or four pans plus a chopping board plus every measuring cup in the kitchen. This skillet dinner has many virtues. The measurements needn't be precise; merely eyeing them is sufficient. You can use up bruised apples or onions, spotty cabbage, and cider that's passed the point of "liquid refreshment." You can halve the meat or double the cabbage, and you can substitute sausage for beef or use them half and half. If you want, serve a green vegetable on the side, or lay out bread and cheese. Either way, you have what dieticians call a well-balanced meal.

Cabbage Skillet Dinner

1 pound ground beef
¾ cup chopped onion
1 cup cider or apple juice
2 cups chopped cabbage
2 large cooking apples cored but unpeeled, cubed
2 tablespoons brown sugar or honey
1 teaspoon salt
½ teaspoon caraway seeds
½ teaspoon pepper

Brown beef and onion until onion is tender. Drain off drippings. Add everything else. Heat to boiling, then lower to a simmer and cook, uncovered, for 25 to 30 minutes until apples are tender and most of the liquid has evaporated. Serves 4 to 6.

This next recipe is not quite so virtuous. You can still play fast and loose with the ingredients—halving the meat or using beef instead of sausage, adding celery or peas—but this recipe requires time on the stove as well as in the oven. Save it for a cold winter evening, when the warmth it gives your kitchen justifies the extra heat and cooking time. The recipe calls for a pie pan, but if I had one of those Corning-type skillets for use on oven and range, I'd adjust the proportions and save my husband the bother of an extra pan to wash. The recipe as I found it called for covering the filling with pie pastry or quick puff pastry. For simplicity's sake, use biscuit dough. Serve applesauce for dessert.

Meat and Cabbage Pie

1 pound Polish sausage in slices ½ inch
   thick
1 onion, chopped or sliced
1 head cabbage, chopped (green is better)
1 teaspoon caraway seeds
1 teaspoon sugar
2 tablespoons lemon juice
salt and pepper to taste (and maybe some
   dill)
1 potato, shredded or diced
biscuit dough

Brown meat. Drain grease and add onion. Cook until tender, not brown, and add cabbage, caraway, sugar, and lemon. Add salt and pepper to taste. Cover and cook for 5 minutes. Add potato and cook another 12 to 15 minutes. Put your mixture in an oven-proof pan (if it's not in one already) and cover with dough. Bake in a hot oven (400 to 425°F) for about 15 minutes, until biscuits are done.

You can always serve cabbage in soup, preferably a wonderfully creamy version. I don't offer any recipes because several are easily available in cookbooks. Instead, here's the soup that got us, as newlywed students, through many a cold and penniless month. Served with a whole-grain bread with lots of crunch and a thick slice of cheese, there's no better winter supper. My well-seasoned copy of *The New York Times Large Type Cookbook* opens right to it.

Corn Chowder

½ pound salt pork, diced
¼ cup chopped onion
½ cup chopped celery
¼ cup chopped green pepper
1 cup diced raw potatoes
salt and black pepper
3 tablespoons flour
2 cups milk
2 cups freshly cut corn (I use canned)
2 cups water
2 teaspoons turmeric (I substitute curry)
½ bay leaf
2 tablespoons chopped parsley

1) Sauté salt pork until crisp and golden. Add onion and celery; cook until tender but

not browned. Add green pepper, potatoes, water, turmeric, bay leaf, salt, and pepper. Simmer 20 minutes, until potatoes are *barely* tender.

2) Mix flour with ½ cup milk. Heat remaining milk and add to blended flour. Stir into hot soup and heat, stirring until mixture thickens. Add corn and parsley.

3) Cook about 4 minutes. Check seasoning.

Serves 8. (Or so the recipe says. My husband and I usually finished a batch in two evenings.)

One last meal-in-one; remember it when you pause by those expensive and gimmicky "helpers" and "starters" at the grocery. This one's better, faster, easier, cheaper. It's as comforting on a cold night as its name implies it might be. I found it in our local newspaper's recipe-exchange column.

Mother's Winter Soup

1 pound ground beef
1 large onion, chopped
16-ounce package frozen vegetables (or canned equivalent)
16-ounce can whole tomatoes, chopped
4 cups beef broth or bouillon
1 clove garlic, minced
1 bay leaf
1 teaspoon oregano
½ teaspoon salt
pepper to taste
1 cup broken spaghetti
1 tablespoon lemon juice
sour cream for topping

Brown beef and onion in a large saucepan. Drain off drippings. Add remaining ingredients, except lemon juice, spaghetti, and sour cream. Bring to a boil. Reduce heat and simmer 45 minutes. Add broken spaghetti and simmer for 15 minutes more or until pasta is cooked. Salt and pepper to taste. Just before serving, stir in lemon juice. Top each individual bowl with a dollop of sour cream. Makes 4 to 6 servings.

My family's not real keen on fish. Their comments are always politely complimentary when I serve it, but I've noticed they don't pester me to serve it often. That's okay, considering the way fish prices are accelerating. Fresh fish doesn't keep well, anyway, and frozen is virtually tasteless. Here's a recipe that accepts fresh or frozen equally well. It's tasty, fast, and cheap, assuming you get a good buy on fish.

The name, I realize, is as eclectic as the ingredients. It is my own, to the sorrow—but not surprise—of my Latin and French teachers. The original name was unacceptable. Once they try it, guests like it, but I was getting a 100 percent refusal rate to the invitation, "By the way, can't you stay for supper? We're having ____." Since I changed the name, I've had no refusals. Of course, I've had no multilingual guests either. The original name? My secret.

Piscis en mélange

2 tablespoons cooking oil or baking grease
1 clove garlic, minced (optional)*
4 or 5 potatoes, diced but unpeeled
1 onion, coarsely chopped
salt and pepper to taste

1 pound cheap, firm white fish, cut into
  bite-size cubes (¾ pounds is okay)
*occasional, optional flavor—curry or dill

When the oil is very hot in your frying pan,
add potatoes and garlic. Turn potatoes
frequently until they're partially crusty but
not cooked through. They may sound like
they're burning. Add onions, green pepper,
salt, and pepper. Cover the pan and let contents cook at reduced heat for two or three
minutes. Mix in fish, cover, and cook for
about five minutes. The diced potatoes will
be barely tender and the fish cooked through.

Chicken recipes can be found by the dozen these
days, so I won't go into them. For a different reason
I'll *almost* skip desserts. These I make so seldom that
I don't begrudge my sweet tooth the expense of time
or trouble. One dessert, however, I must mention in
some detail.

I had bought for ninety-nine cents a half-bushel
of slightly bruised apples the grocery couldn't sell at
regular price. I lugged them home, thinking apple
dumplings, applesauce, and, for dinner that first
night, an apple crisp recipe I had discovered several
days earlier among some old and yellowing clippings. But search as I might, I couldn't find that
recipe again anywhere. The thought that I might
have to find a substitute, might have to start checking the indexes of my five-foot row of cookbooks was
out of the question.

There were just three papers left in the stack of
clippings and scribbles. All of them were yellow
legal-size, definitely not the raggedy-edged two-
by-three for which I was looking. But at the top of the
top legal-size page, hastily copied from a book of

home-style, Nova Scotia recipes, was a recipe for Levi's Pie, parenthetically labeled "apple crisp"! Not only did my family lick the pan clean, but at the church potluck dinner to which I took a doubled recipe the next night, it was the undisputed favorite. The recipe was so simple it was still in my head; I wrote it down on a scrap of paper which was passed around the room and copied quickly. There are only six ingredients, and if you're any good with a paring knife you can put the recipe together in nearly as few minutes as it takes to copy it. Well, give yourself ten minutes.

Levi's Pie (or Apple Crisp)

4 to 6 medium apples
¾ cup rolled oats
¾ cup brown sugar
½ cup flour
1 teaspoon cinnamon
½ cup butter

Pare apples and slice thin. Arrange in greased baking dish. Combine dry ingredients and mix well. Cut in the butter. Sprinkle this mixture over apples. Bake in a moderate oven, 350°F for 35 to 40 minutes. Serve warm (maybe with whipped cream, ice cream, or a cold glass of milk.)

These dozen or so recipes aren't enough to keep your family or yourself satisfied night after night, week after week. But they're proof that everyday cooking need not be expensive or time-consuming to be tasty. More necessary than cash or labor is a bit of thought. Sometimes this boils down to the conclusion that a whole new approach to cooking and eating is the only solution. This can occur gradually and without pain. Here's a jambalaya of ways to combine those two worthy adages, "waste not, want not" and "less is more."

Try stir-fry, Chinese-style without chopsticks. Two pork chops do the work of three. One small steak does the work of two. Cut the meat into bite-size chunks (no larger or they'll be gobbled down unchewed and unappreciated). Fry the chunks quickly (woks are good but inessential) in just enough heated oil to keep them from burning. Remove them to a platter, heat more oil, and similarly quick-fry some chopped vegetables of your preference. Celery, peas, beans, broccoli stems, green peppers are the usual ones. Lettuce and cabbage cores, grated, are not so expected, and will almost pass for water chestnuts (too expensive for a budget meal). Serve with rice or with potato chunks boiled (skins left on).

Next time you make mashed potatoes, keep the potato peels. Within a week or so, chop them coarsely and quick-fry in pork fat or butter. At the last moment before serving, garnish with chopped scallions or parsley.

Save the rinds from citrus fruit. Use slivers of the peel everywhere: in poultry, on cooked vegetables, in a salad of grapefruit-orange-green peppers, on broiled chicken, in rice, with nuts and chocolate bits in ice cream.

Don't let food spoil. Americans "tithe" their food budget: one tenth of what we buy goes into the garbage. Store legumes and grains in tightly closed jars in cool, dark places. Some grain products keep best in the freezer. Lemons and limes have a longer refrigerator life if kept in a tightly closed jar. Parsley and watercress stay fresh if kept in a tightly closed jar, with an inch or so of water for the stems to stand in. Extend the life of garlic by skinning each clove and storing in a tiny, refrigerated jar of corn oil; when the cloves are used up, use the oil for cooking. Keep all but a few days' worth of your precious and costly olive oil in a dark jar in the refrigerator. If a food product has storage instructions, heed them.

When something starts to "go," remove the bad portion and use the rest immediately. Here's a recipe for using up wilted lettuce in a tasty way. It comes from a lady in her eighties who lets nothing from her five gardens go to waste.

> Fry 4 to 6 slices of bacon and one medium onion (sliced) until cooked but not crisp. Pour off the fat except for about 2 tablespoons. Add 1 tablespoon sugar and ½ tablespoon salt. Keep this combination hot until you're ready to serve the meal, at which time you add your lettuce (as much as you want, however wilted) and toss lightly.

When bananas begin to turn black, throw them, unpeeled, into the freezer to accumulate. They're fine for bread or muffins or your next batch of pancake batter.

Learn to cut up your own chicken. That six cents a pound difference doesn't seem like much, but it amounts to a free chicken per month at the rate we consume it. Freeze the innards and bony sections until you have a plastic bagful. Then add a carrot or two, a chopped onion, a clove of garlic, some old celery, and lots of herbs, and cook down in a huge pot or two of water. You'll have plenty of meat for a couple meals of creamed chicken, enough extra meat for some soup, plus a month's worth of chicken stock.

For a wonderful cream of chicken recipe, find

the More-With-Less Cookbook by Doris Janzen Long-acre ($3.95 from Bantam Books). Follow her advice, and the book will pay for itself in less than a week. I like her recipes because most of them are as fast and easy as they are cheap. Her book discusses grains and legumes without sounding as if she's preaching from an "organic" pulpit. Soybeans, after all, are soybeans; you like 'em or you don't. But the real reason I like her cookbook, as you'll discover if you read it with extreme care, is a recipe for—are you ready?—pumpkin leaves! Look carefully; that recipe didn't make the index.

Another cookbook is Keep It Simple, 30-Minute Meals from Scratch ($3.95 from Pocket Books). Marian Burros is a working mother who knows the limits of time and money but appreciates tasty food that's healthy, too. I wish I'd said everything she's said about the "American Food Industry." Her first book was Pure and Simple. I'd trade every cookbook in our house (excepting Maida Heatter's Book of Great Cookies) for the two books I've just mentioned.

Plan up to an egg a day per person in your household. Eggs are cheap, and fresh-from-the-farm eggs last for at least a month, properly stored. Ounce for ounce, assume the larger sizes to be cheaper—unless there's more than a ten-cent spread between consecutive sizes.

Eat lots of cheap protein in the form of quiche, but don't blow it all by using those store-bought, frozen pie shells. Many quiche recipes taste perfectly fine without a crust. Experiment. Sometimes I prefer a crust, but the thought of rolling one out as often as we eat quiche is not something I hanker to do. So I plan ahead and make several crusts at once, then pull them out of the freezer as I need them.

When you use the oven, especially in summertime, cook several things simultaneously or in quick succession. For instance, if you're making beans that must slow cook for several hours, roast chicken to eat cold another day, bake pie shells to freeze, make a rice pudding to serve at the same meal with the beans—providing cheap "complementary protein." (For more "cheap protein" ideas, see the Longacre book mentioned above.)

Halve your milk bill but not with the extender that is "instant." It tastes horrible, is grainy, and constantly needs shaking (which means lids flying and milk spilling everywhere)—a real mess. Get dry milk powder which does not say "instant" but works quickly enough and tastes like the real stuff. Mix it half and half with regular milk if you're not crazy about the taste. I'm lazy; I pay $3.30 for a one-pound bag of nonfat dry milk powder at a convenient local store. I could buy a different brand through the mail for $1.97 ($2.40 for whole, $1.80 for butter, 84¢ for whey) and cut our milk bill even further. Write to Walnut Acres, Penns Creek, Pennsylvania 17862 for a catalog. If, for some reason, you should not like the taste of that or any brand you first try, keep trying other brands. Not all taste the same.

Use lots of herbs. Better to serve a humble food perfectly made than a costly one with no flavor. But avoid those little jars and tiny cans; what you pay for is the package. Herbs available by the ounce, in bulk, are much cheaper. Since certain ones lose their intensity through this exposure, sniff before you scoop.

Grow some of your own herbs. Many are perennials. I planted an eighty-nine cent mint plant three years ago. Since then, I've used it every day in season and supplied our whole neighborhood. The same is true of thyme I started. Our backyard is, literally, thyme. We got rid of the grass—keeping a mower for a spot no bigger than the floor of a room seemed silly—and replaced it with thyme plantings of a variety that can bear trampling. Need I say we use thyme to flavor nearly everything? Plant parsley in a place protected from the elements, and you may need to reseed only every two or three years; our parsley season lasts from Easter until Christmas.

Grow a garden. It needn't be big. Buy a couple of five-dollar half-barrels or scrounge their equivalent; they're deep enough so you don't have to water constantly. Plant simple things whose harvests overlap: peas, lettuce, parsley, spinach, a few beets, green beans, one zucchini plant, one or two cucumber plants, and a few container tomatoes that you stake in the center. Don't forget basil; this herb and tomatoes get along as well together in dirt as they do on the table. Solicit free advice from neighbors and local gardeners. Borrow a book from the library; there are dozens geared especially for beginning gardeners with little space and even less cash. For a fifteen-dollar investment you can reap a return of fresh produce worth ten times that much.

Buy some products cooperatively. I don't belong to an official food co-op, at times rather complicated business ventures, but occasionally I'll go together with a friend or two to buy in quantity. That way we find quality we could not afford individually. Once a year a friend and I order several pounds of dried fruit straight from the source, a farm in California. The same fruits bought locally in little packages would cost three times what we pay. Plus ours are fresher and sweeter than those in the stores. Sometimes we do the same thing with foods grown closer to home. Who can use up, before it rots, a bushel of grapes, for instance? Our dried fruit source is Benech Farms of Almaden, 20250 McKean Rd.,

P.O. Box 6387, San Jose, California 95150.

Waste no more money on those "cream of" x-brand soups. Tastier homemade versions require only one or two minutes more than it takes to open a can. I make a combination roux/white sauce this way: Melt one, two, three !or however many) tablespoons of margarine or butter. *Quickly* stir or whisk in an equal (or slightly lesser) amount of flour. Immediately but gradually add as much of the milk or stock as you want, stirring (the whole thirty seconds or so!) until you reach the desired consistency. That's it! If you want cheese flavor, stir in, near the end, some grated cheese. If you want onion or mushroom or celery or such, put that ingredient in, finely chopped, between the butter and flour steps. Onion is a good addition anytime.

Don't pay for convenience or packaging. Homemade croutons take five minutes to make. They're free if you use leftover toast and the heels of bread that would otherwise be tossed away. They taste better too. If you like the standard measurement of individually boxed cereals, put a plastic measuring cup in the big cereal box. Better yet, buy the cereal in bulk and keep it in jars. Here's my case study: Just trying them out, I recently paid $1.09 for eight one-ounce packets of a flavored instant oatmeal. Also in my cupboard is a cylindrical package by the same manufacturer. It holds the same product but with no flavoring. The cost of the cylindrical version?—eighteen ounces for seventy-nine cents. Beside it sits a jar filled with the same food, 100 percent rolled oats, bought in bulk from a barrel where I scooped it out—two pounds for eighty-nine cents. We buy rice, popcorn, legumes, and grain the same way. Part of the secret to this kind of buying is finding the right place to shop for the best values in bulk buying, seldom your neighborhood supermarket franchise. Health-food shops are often prohibitive in cost. The co-op store where I buy mine requires no membership, no obligations, no commitments. It is a commercial venture that welcomes the public. It did, however, take me a while to find it, so you may have to look around, too.

Remember that the most tempting of the convenience foods are also the most price-inflated. You can delude your conscience into smug satisfaction by settling for the store's second-best, telling yourself that spending even a little bit less money justifies your purchase. Or you can make, for half the cost, a version superior to any the store offers. Take Boursin, that creamy, spicy cheese of French origin. Our typical American versions pale in comparison to what one finds in France. Even worse are the American substitutes for the substitutes. Yet their taste is tempting enough to *dissolve* all my *resolve*. I try to remember that my friend Marjery has a Boursin recipe that takes three minutes. Mix together all of the following: 8 ounces cream cheese (at room temperature), 1 clove minced garlic, ¼ to ½ tablespoon dry mustard, 2 teaspoons dill weed, 1 teaspoon parsley flakes, 1 to 2 teaspoons Italian herbs (tarragon, oregano, etc.), salt or 1 to 2 teaspoons McCormick's Season-All (keep it on hand for just this use!), red wine vinegar to taste (about 1 tablespoon or a little less). *Voilà!* While you sit back and savor your Boursin on a cracker, remind yourself that living poor doesn't have to taste bad!

7

100,000 Miles? That's Nothing!

The way of the sluggard is blocked with thorns, but the path of the upright is a highway.

PROVERBS 15:19

Cars! They might as well be houses, the way they guzzle money. Tune-ups, tires, insurance, taxes: those are the *predictable* expenses, *above* the cost of the car itself. Then come batteries, bumpers, belts, and breakdowns! Cars are not the only thing wrong with our society, but their role as villain is large. Most of us must place no small amount of reliance on this machine that controls us even as it rests in the mechanic's garage. After sixty-plus years of an automotive America, the situation is not improving. If anything, it's becoming worse. As long as there are cars, there will be unsolvable problems. Witness my own.

We bought our Omni new in 1978, its first year of manufacture. We bought it to replace our '71 Volkswagen which looked every bit its age: scarred body, bald spots (even in the floor), bent frame, and vital parts so weary they truly couldn't be expected to travel another mile. It had had a hard life with us and died an unnecessarily early death. Fearing the safety of some innocent buyer who might dare to keep it on the road, we gave it to the automotive department of a local high school and claimed the tax deduction for a charitable contribution. Our next car, we determined, we'd give a better chance at longevity. The new Omni, from all available evidence, looked like a good choice. We would have preferred to wait a year, give the engineers at Dodge time to iron out kinks that are inevitable in every car model's first year, but the "bug" in the alley denied us that choice. We had to have a car. We gambled and bought the Omni. So much for gambling!

In 1978, Detroit (by that I mean the U.S. automotive industry) was just getting into fancy electrical systems—catalytic converters and the like—the nemesis of many a late-model car and its owner, including myself. The more technologically tricky an object is, the greater the chance for breakdown. The greater the breakdowns, the greater the amount of energy wasted in frustration. (To say nothing of cash!) That's both fact and E. F. Schumacher theory.

We had electrical problems practically from day one. Before that new-car odor had disappeared, the Omni was back at the dealer's. The problem, they said, was a single but crucial bolt. They thought they'd fixed it. So did we. Off we went for the weekend, an all-night ride up to western New York for some clean autumn air and several swallows of fresh-pressed apple cider. The seven-hour ride is dark and swift, just vehicles and the Pennsylvania forest. Breakdowns can be lonely. After Harrisburg, there's virtually nothing open en route but a few truck stops and one donut shop.

Just south of Harrisburg our lights started to dim, the green glow of the dashboard becoming more and more faint. There was no question. It was the electrical system. Exactly what *part* of that system we didn't know. Why should we? The "experts" evidently didn't. The hour was near midnight. Should we look for a motel? Dare we pull over until dawn, the three of us huddled together under the single emergency blanket we always carry? Could the driver of one of those big rigs help if we waved him down? We reached the outskirts of Harrisburg and began to look for an appropriate parking spot, one where we'd feel safe and from which we could hike, come daylight, to a garage. There was our spot, the parking lot of a miserable-looking auto repair shop, dark now.

But wait! There was a light! In the back room, the sole owner-cum-mechanic was sharing a few Friday night beers with a friend. We explained the problem, and the old man grunted understandingly: "These newfangled engines! Why couldn't they recognize a good thing when they had it—hang onto the old slant-six?" He could promise nothing, but two hours later we were on our way, our checking account down about fifty dollars and no hope of recovery under warranty coverage. The rest of the weekend was wonderful, but every hundred miles or so we had to check on that bolt. Yep, the same "crucial" bolt.

Home again, back we went to the dealer. "Fixed!" they told us triumphantly. But a few months later, and again a few months after that—the same problem, always in the most remote of areas and after midnight or on weekends. We tried a different dealer. We tried the "independents." By this time it was not the expense so much as the frustration. I dreaded the daily rides home from work. Would I make it? A couple of times I couldn't even make it out of the parking garage. I had to be towed.

By now the car was nearly three years old. The warranty, for what it had been worth, was long gone. We could use legal recourse to get free repairs, but how were they going to repair something they evidently couldn't find? Remaining were but two car payments. Jack talked more and more angrily about getting rid of the Omni. But for what? And how? This was a mere two months before my last paycheck. It and our final car payment would coincide. Should we trade the headache of the Omni's repairs for a bigger one of debt? Debt on a new car that might have its own headaches?

Our second set of front shocks were, apparently,

111

going. Sounds from the front end were ominous. On a "regular" car shocks aren't bad—seventy-five dollars maximum. Omni's have MacArthur struts—replacing a set costs nearly two hundred dollars. The mechanic had muffed our first replacement. Realizing that a couple of months later, we took the car back to the same garage; the ownership had changed.

Nor did the doors work properly. First one, then another; sometimes from the inside, sometimes from the outside: they wouldn't open.

Jack's anger grew. Maybe it *was* throwing good money after bad to keep the car. But what was our alternative?

A few evenings later, JC burst into the kitchen. What's this? Baseball games last more than an hour.

"We had an accident!" she exclaimed in delight.

I nodded, mute and numb. Where was Jack? Where was Alexis? Where was the *car*?

"Not so bad," my brother-in-law tried to explain as he followed her in through the back door. "A drunk creamed our backside."

Jack walked in, five-month-old Alexis in his arms. Huge smiles, happy faces. They appeared no worse for wear. But the car? The car? Surely Jack's smile meant it was totaled. The insurance money would be our down payment on a new one.

"Barely dented our fenders," Jack said. "All we *need* to get fixed is the light."

Dented fenders and broken bumpers have never bothered either of us. That's life in the city—cosmetic handicaps. If we worried about our car's appearance, we'd be totally broke. But body damage makes a car less saleable. Most people *mind* dents and bruises. Would we recover our money if we made the repairs and sold the car through the classifieds? The problem was growing more complicated, rather than less. We decided to stall the decision a while. Meantime, I would take the children to visit my sister for a few days and try out the small-town Chrysler-Dodge dealership she described as conscientious, prompt, reliable, efficient, and too good to be true.

What had we to lose? At every right turn, the sound coming from the shocks was a frightening thing to hear. The front tires were nearly bald and state inspection was fast approaching. Plus, I realized (every time I was first in line at the traffic light when it turned green) the dilly-dallying engine meant it was high time for some tuning. Lastly, we had to keep at least *one* lockable door in operation.

Two days, three days, four days in the garage. My suspicions were confirmed. It was with dread that I rode with my sister to pick up the Omni. I envisioned the bill. Five, six, seven hundred dollars. New shocks, new generator, new catalytic converter, new tires. If it was more than four hundred, I decided in a rush, I would ask how much they'd give me toward a trade-in. Nearly sick to my stomach, I walked into the garage trying to remind myself that I was a grown woman and these were the realities of life.

"Hi. Mine's the green Omni with the rack on top." I pointed feebly in its direction. "Find the trouble . . . troubles?" I'd explained the electrical problem when we took it in.

"Sure did. You certainly had a *lot* of them." I groaned at his cheerfulness; the steak on his table that night would be on this sucker from the city.

"Here it is." He put the yellow paper down on the counter in front of me. "Sorry it's so high. We put in already-used parts where we could."

His monologue sounded so familiar I could have

recited it myself. Oh, well. There was nothing to do but open my eyes. The figure I saw was $281. I scanned the bill. Surely that wasn't the *bottom* line? Indeed it was.

"Didn't you ever get a recall for that electrical system?" I was being asked. "The dealer where you bought it should have made this replacement long ago. No matter, I'll send the papers through. They all go to the same place anyway. That part of the cost is on Chrysler."

I started to write the check, making some remark about the shocks costing only sixty dollars. Had they perhaps decided not to do them?

"Oh, yes," he said, turning toward the counter behind him. He held out a super-sized sort of spring. "This is all that was the matter. Sorry we couldn't fix it. We had to put in a secondhand extra we had hanging around. That's that sixteen dollars you see noted. The rest of the cost is labor; those buggers take the better part of a day to get at."

You should have heard my prayers *that* night! And again a few weeks later. . . .

The insurance papers took a few weeks to be processed, but finally the check arrived. It was for $281!!!

That's still not the end of the story. A few weeks later, my husband told a friend of ours, an attorney who works for an insurance company, about the accident; the driver who caused it was not only drunk and driving—unlicensed—a car with no brakes, but he was uninsured. Under our state's uninsured motorist law, our friend told us, there's a little-known clause that says the innocent party is due the hundred-dollar deductible that we would have had to pay had we had the accident damage repaired, fixed those cosmetic blemishes we chose to ignore.

One quick call to our insurer's attorney and that money, too, was ours.

It's nearly a year later now. We've had no mechanical troubles to date. Okay, the front door on the driver's side needs a new "rubber band" to operate properly, but that's an inconvenience with which I can live. Meantime, another Omni episode is in the offing.

Two weeks ago we received a letter from Chrysler Corporation. Jack, providentially, checked the mail that night; I'd have thrown the letter away, unopened, enraged at the nerve of their local dealers trying to solicit further business from us. It was a recall notice—the second one, they claimed—for the car part that cost us so much misery and expense. (It *had* been more than a bolt, but this was not their way of phrasing it, of course.) Jack thinks we may have legal recourse. I'm sure we do; filed away carefully are all our auto expense records. But guess what I'm going to do instead? I'm going to send Chrysler chronologically arranged duplicates of all our repair records, enclosing the kindest, most thought-out letter I've ever composed. If I were a betting person, I'd say our next year's car expenses will pretty much "take care of themselves"!

Meantime, I have hoses and air filters and PCV valves to keep me busy. I'm not an under-the-hood mechanic. I have neither the skills nor the special tools most late-model cars require. My role is to keep an educated eye on the system, to keep what things I can from going wrong and to spot small, inexpensive problems before they become major, costly ones. My job, in other words, is preventive maintenance. This Omni can travel over 100,000 miles—if I can slow the aging process that would stop us short of that goal.

WHITE-GLOVE MAINTENANCE

So simple that many folks underestimate its value is keeping the car in one piece. Many a car has gone to an early grave not because the engine parts were irreparable, but because the body simply fell apart. Also, the itch for a new car may not be so intense if you keep the car you have in reasonably attractive shape. That you should rustproof (do not confuse with undercoating) a new car goes without saying. But if you're reading this book, chances are that it's too late for that $100 to $200 investment to be worthwhile; there's good reason rustproofers don't give older cars full warranties. The next best thing—and one you should do anyway—is to be conscientious about cleaning. A thorough job once a season (four times yearly) is more effective than a twenty-minute hosedown once a month. Find a slightly shaded spot and plan on spending a couple of hours there. If you're using a do-it-yourself car wash, do the first couple steps at home and return home for the waxing.

During this cleaning, you may notice nicks and bruises that have managed, these many months, to evade your eye—or that you preferred not to acknowledge. Hie yourself to an auto-supply shop or to a dealership's parts department where you can make a paint match. Don't let them tell you, unless yours is a *very* old car, that your shade isn't available. Manufacturers have coded every color and marked this code in a standard place. The standard place, unfortunately, varies by manufacturer (check your owner's manual first). If you don't know where to look and the shop clerks don't either, they *can* look it up, even order it if necessary. You needn't drive a pimpled car. Once you have your paint (a vial resembling nail polish with a brush in the bottle—

costs about $5), use steel wool or emery on the blemishes, feathering onto the good paint. Remove all dust. Brush on a thin layer of rust-inhibiting primer. Allow it to dry thoroughly before you apply the first of several layers of your color. Make each layer thin (tougher and no drips) and a day or so apart, until the newly painted surface is level with the old. Rub on a little wax and you're finished.

> Flood the car with water that is *not* under high pressure (which could push the dirt deep into the paint); save the high pressure for the rinse. Apply car soap undiluted (no dish detergent or under-the-counter cleaners, please!) to presoak the worst parts: fenders (inside and outside) and those pitted-looking areas under the doors and bumpers. Now you're ready for the big scrub. Make it gentle, heeding the manufacturer's instructions on your car soap. The water you use to rinse should be as high-pressured as you can get it. In rinsing, you will start with the car's top and end by giving special attention to the parts that are the most crucial but the most frequently overlooked: the insides of the fenders and the auto's undersides. Don't bother with a pricey chamois for drying; old terrycloth is better anyway. Next, you're ready to wax. Again, keep your touch gentle and don't neglect the chrome (stainless steel you can ignore). After you clean the vinyl seats inside, give them a spray of silicone-based conditioner (available in an auto-supply shop). Spray the same stuff on the weather stripping around the doors.

Much of the care that keeps a car running is as simple as the labor that prevents it from rusting away. The oldest cars I know have owners who are diligent about tending the oil. They check it every time they fill the gas tank. They change the filter every time they change the oil, which is every two thousand to four thousand miles, *no matter what the owner's manual recommends.*

Checking the oil is a cinch; do it after the engine has been warmed by several miles of running. If you don't even know where the dipstick is, next time you ask the station attendant to check it, get out of the car and observe carefully. This is all he does: remove the dipstick, wipe it clean, note the mark (notches or words) where the oil should reach, put the dipstick back in *all* the way, and pull it out again to see the actual oil level. If it needs a quart, add a quart. If it needs a quart and a half, add a quart and a half. Don't try to add two. Oil is one of those things of which too much is almost as bad as too little. What oil? Not the cheap stuff. Check the can's top for SE (not SAE which is something else) and numbers that match the ones your owner's manual recommends. Those numbers refer to viscosity or weight; the SE means the oil has ingredients that protect against corrosion and oxidation. The only tools you'll need are a clean rag and a spout for the oil can. (Please dispose of your oil cans properly. Tote them to your gas station's trash next time you fill up, or follow the advice of your community's sanitation administrator, but *do not* throw oil cans in trash to be used for landfill or put the cans anywhere the oil might harm vegetation or get into a water supply.)

Changing the oil and oil filter are simple, too, but not so simple as merely upending a can over the right hole under the hood. Those jobs are, therefore, beyond the scope of this book. When you're ready to change the oil yourself, there are dozens of car manuals eager to show you how; nearly any one of them has recommendable, easy-to-follow instructions.

Keeping your tires adequately and evenly inflated takes only minutes a month but can drop your fuel bill by dollars—not pennies—in that time. Also, the tires last longer. Buy a tire gauge; those on air pumps are notoriously unreliable. (You don't need a twenty-dollar model but you do want one good enough to be reliable.) Check the tires when they're cold. That's also the way they should be when you add air, so locate a pump within two or three miles of your house. Both your owner's manual and a marker on or around the driver's door can tell you how much air the manufacturer thinks you need. Add a couple of pounds for further savings in gas mileage; you may have a slightly bumpy ride but not dangerously so. Some pros recommend increasing the pressure by five pounds on some tires. Some pros also recommend that you check your tires weekly. Let's be realistic: that may be a good idea if you put hundreds of miles on your car each week or if the weather dictates (tires lose a pound or two of pressure for every ten degrees Fahrenheit the temperature drops), but under normal circumstances twice monthly is sufficient. Don't overinflate (you'll wear out the center tread) or underinflate (the edges will wear too fast).

A side note on tires: Keep your wheels balanced and your front end aligned. It takes only a few thousand miles to wear out a pair of tires if this isn't done. To save money, don't have the front end aligned until you're sure the problem is not unbalanced wheels—a less expensive problem. Have this check done at least twice yearly, one of those times being right after "pothole" season. Balancing your wheels and, in nearly all cases, aligning the front end costs considerably less than a new set of tires, and you'll get improved mileage.

Batteries seem to be a common and a constant

problem, so much so that people accept the fact that their car "needs" a new battery every two or three years. It need not be so, even with those sealed, "lifetime" batteries that last about as long as their three- or five-year warranties, which buyers realize too late are pro rata. When you must replace your battery and you plan on making your car last a good while, get the best you can afford. If you're spending the kind of money required for a *low*-maintenance, *low*-antimony battery, take the next step: buy a battery that's maintenance-*free*, antimony-*free*. Look for a battery warranted for as long as you own your car, although there aren't many of this type still available. If your car is getting up there in years, buy a battery with a little extra oomph, a slightly larger cubic-inch-capacity (expressed as CCA for "cold cranking amps") than the one you now use. Your starter will love it and you'll have a more dependable car. To make sure that you don't get a battery, whatever the type, stale from a long shelf life, check the date of manufacture. Maintenance-free (but *not* low-maintenance!) are less prone to going stale. Lastly, make sure the mechanic who installs it gives it a long, slow "finish" charge—just in case.

Once it's in, your role is seeing that the battery is kept clean, tight, and properly charged. Undercharge or overcharge, especially in a regular battery, reduces cranking capacity and shortens life, affecting the performance of the rest of the car. Have the charge checked every couple of months. Whenever you check your oil, give a jiggle to the battery to make sure it's tight in its place, and give a glance to make sure the terminals and cable ends are clean. A loose battery will self-destruct internally; make sure the clamps allow no movement. Once cleaned (with baking soda if you feel up to it), the terminals should be coated with a non-metallic grease such as petroleum jelly. Occasionally, if your battery is not the sealed type, check the level of electrolyte: remove the caps one at a time to make sure the electrolyte covers the tops of the little plates you'll see inside. If not, add water; distilled is better than tap (all you're likely to get from a service station).

Another between-tune-ups checkup you can and should do is see that all goes well in the **coolant and radiator.** Most late-model cars have an overflow tank (see-through plastic) marked for levels to check when the engine is warm and when it is cool. If the coolant is low, add a half-and-half mix of water and antifreeze, mixed before you put it in. Check your radiator only when the engine is cold. Even then, take care. Not to scare but to warn, I must relate the last time I did this. I was at a self-service gas station. The attendant, who lent me a rag to check the oil, watched me uneasily. He pointed to a stain on the roof overhead where the radiator cap had landed when another attendant had gotten carelessly hasty the week before. That haste landed the attendant in the hospital with second-degree burns. So . . . remove the cap very slowly, allowing pressure to escape, and keep your head *back*. If, when you run your finger around the inside of the throat, you find grease or rust, it's high time to drain and flush the whole system so that the accumulated crud doesn't hinder circulation and engine performance and ring up a hundred-dollar radiator repair bill. (Coolant costs under five dollars a gallon.) That kind of accumulated crud also indicates that your car is overdue for tuning. Have you noticed a ragged idle, stodgy response, decreasing gas mileage?

Make every dollar of that costly **visit to the mechanic** count. Little things untended can waste precious dollars by preventing the tended items from operating at peak efficiency. A well-tuned car averages at least 5 percent better gas mileage and slows the aging of your car's vital parts. Go to your mechanic informed and prepared. Take a list of specifics instead of requesting a general tune-up. You'll be less likely to get shoddy workmanship and an incomplete job if the mechanic realizes he may be asked, point by point, about work you've specified. This is not being abrasive. It's being businesslike, and a worthy mechanic will appreciate your care. Now to compile a list of what you know needs doing and what you suspect might. First, pull out your owner's manual to see the manufacturer's minimum recommendations for your mileage, and prepare to add to it. Time to take pencil in hand.

Topping your list—you don't even have to check—**is an oil change.** But what if your car's been drinking a little more oil than usual lately? This is common when a tune-up's overdue, but you may have a leak around the gasket. Or what if you've been noticing clouds of blue smoke puff out from your tailpipe as you start up or accelerate? Ask the mechanic to check—and give you an estimate for—valve seals, valve guides, and piston rings. This repair is *way* beyond the scope of a tune-up, but this is the time to define problems you may need to deal with soon.

Check the little plug that is your PCV (positive crankcase valve). The hardest part of checking it is finding it. Once you do, you can untwist it and tell at a glance whether it's clean. A dirty one undoes much of the benefit of a clean air filter. Putting in a new PCV takes the same twenty seconds as replacing the old one. (This is the only do-it-yourself part of this tune-up. The rest is inspection—honest!)

Check the brakes. Push the pedal down. It shouldn't go more than halfway before you feel you're hitting something hard. If it's spongy, you may have air bubbles in the brake lines. If you can push it nearly to the floor, you may have problems in the master cylinder. If your car moves easily in "drive" or "first" (or any other gear!) with the parking brake firm, your parking brake needs work.

Check the cooling system as detailed above. If it's been more than a year since the last flush and refill, it's time for another, whether or not you see crud. Note the spring and seal on each radiator cap; the radiator will not hold pressure if either one has deteriorated, in which case you need replacements. If you see corrosion or streaking (probably white) you no doubt have a leak.

Check your battery as described above. Make a note to have the charge checked and the battery cleaned off and filled if you're not up to that task.

Check hoses and wires. You want strong, corrosion-free clamps, no frayed or cracked or bulging hoses. Drag out your flashlight so you can note which ones appear bad (even if you don't know where they lead or what they're for), then point them out to the mechanic. The same is true of wires. You can wipe the grime and corrosion off them or leave it for the mechanic to do. If you see corrosion, the connections may need tightening.

Check any belt you see. If it's slick or splitting or peeling it needs to be replaced. To check a belt's tension, find the midpoint (estimated) and push gently. If the belt is shorter than eighteen inches, you should be able to push a maximum of one-quarter inch; if longer than eighteen inches, one-half inch.

Checking the fluids is probably something you

leave **for the mechanic** to do. These are the **ones to mark down on the list:** transmission fluid and filter, power-steering fluid (if appropriate), brake fluid, oil in the differential. Also mark down the gas filter, air filter (and pump), fuel filter (and pump). If you've noticed drips on your driveway, spread some paper under your car at night, after the engine has cooled. If the drip is way toward the front, it's probably your coolant; if it's black and slightly back, suspect motor oil; if brownish red and toward the rear, suspect your transmission fluid. (Your transmission fluid and filter should be changed every two years; such infrequent checks means they are easily forgotten entirely until it's too late.)

A few other basics should be **on the list for the mechanic** to check: alternator (and the rest of the electrical system), ignition coil, manifold heat control valve, carburetor, starter, automatic choke (if appropriate) evaporative control canister. If you don't have electronic ignition, mark down points, rotor, and condenser. Not to be forgotten are the spark plugs. Sometimes they only need filing, but no mechanic is likely to take the time. Replace them, probably every 5,000 miles of city driving or 10,000 miles if most of your driving is on a highway. It's a fact that a single misfiring spark plug can reduce fuel efficiency *at least* 25 percent in a six-cylinder car, even more in a four-cylinder car.

Give your list (keep a duplicate, dated) **to the mechanic** who will work on the car, not to the go-between out front who takes the keys. This may be difficult, but you have everything to gain and nothing to lose. Let the mechanic know of your resolve to stretch every mile possible out of this car. Your list and well-tended car will underscore your sincerity. Your list will be one of symptoms; let the mechanic be the doctor, the one to diagnose the problem and recommend a cure. Don't choose the busiest times for your visits (normally, Monday, Friday, and Saturday are busy) or be in a rush. If your mechanic doesn't know enough to recognize a good and regular customer, find a different mechanic.

That's not easy. I know through experience. Some people swear by mechanics who are certified by various societies. This is, of course, some assurance, but many of those societies' educational courses stress a specialty which may or may not be appropriate to the needs of your car. Sometimes the mechanic who works on your car is not the one whose certificate hangs on the office wall. I prefer word-of-mouth advice from someone with an aged car that's not spent too many days of its life at the shop. If you can get the advice of somebody who "knows cars," so much the better. But get to know your mechanic by name and send a card at Christmas. Establish this kind of relationship and the mechanic is likely to come right out and tell you when you need specialized work, such as on your brakes or transmission, more appropriately done someplace other than that garage. A good mechanic likes to be thought of as more than a mere grease monkey; respect merits respect. Between the two of you, you and your mechanic can hold off the bank-account benders—transmission, engine, differential, and the like—by properly caring for the everyday and not so everyday—alternator, starter coil, pumps, etc.

Getting the car repaired once a part has gone bad is tricky business. A long-established, trusting relationship with a valued and competent mechanic is your best resource. When you take the car in, have marked on paper just when your particular problem occurs: at night? when you turn left? only in rain? when you brake? Remind the mechanic of your financial situation and of the fact that you want to make the car last. Ask if used parts are appropriate and available. If the reply is yes to the first question but no to the second, ask the mechanic if, assuming you can locate the parts, he (or she) would mind using them. There are plenty of used-car lots that exist for the sole purpose of selling parts, many of which come from insurance "wrecks" and are perfectly usable. Owners of these lots know their competition, so prices in any given local area are likely to be similar. You needn't race from lot to lot, comparison shopping. Try calling ahead. Beware of warranties. Also, beware of rebuilt parts, such as batteries and carburetors, that come packaged as new but most definitely *are not anything like new*.

If, after you drive your car home from the shop, you still have trouble, take it back *immediately*— and be nice. Garage folk are immune to tantrums and harangues. What gets results is polite understanding. After all, they want to keep a loyal customer, and the problem may be a minor one.

But what if the problem is major? What if the problems are multiple, and to repair all of them would be costly? Perhaps those necessary repairs aren't worth your trouble and expense. Someone with the time and a mechanical inclination may be able to keep your car operating at a reasonable cost, but you can't. Then it's time to let the car go and put the money you get for it into a replacement. Assuming your car's not a total "goner," there are some things you can do to show it at its best.

Potential buyers, whether they know what they're looking for or not, tend to look under the hood. Let them see you've taken care of the engine. Clean it. Get rid of any dead (or live!) insects and other debris. Cover the distributor and coil (so they don't get wet) and then degrease the engine with a can of cleaner you buy at an auto parts shop. Check (and fill if necessary) the coolant, oil, windshield washer, and battery. Clean off the battery terminals and have the oil changed if it's dirty.

Eliminate as many funny sounds as you can, but don't spend a lot of money. Oil all hinges. Then clean and wax as if you were going on parade; you *are*. Don't forget the trunk. Touch up scratches and rust spots with paint.

You're ready to set a price. Check your library or ask your friendly neighborhood banker if you can look at the latest N.A.D.A. *Official Used Car Guide*, *Black Book Official Used-Car Market Guide*, and *Kelley Blue Book Market Report*. In each of these three books you'll see average wholesale and retail prices and adjustments for high and low mileage. Also, keep an eye on the local paper's classifieds to see what other sellers are asking. When you advertise, be specific. Include the make, model, year, number of cylinders, and any options such as power steering, tinted glass, roof rack. Mention the condition only if it's at least "very good" considering its age, and treat the mileage similarly. Be fair with the price but leave room for bargaining. Let all comers go for a test ride but go with them. As well as answering their questions, *subtly* let them know the careful maintenance you've given the car (if you have!): how frequent and regular the oil changes and tune-ups, parts you've replaced and when—the sort of information you'd like to have if you were shopping. Which you undoubtedly will be soon.

New cars average nearly $9000. The average

monthly payment on a forty-eight month loan at 15 percent approaches $250. Your best bet may be in the secondhand market. Some perfectly fine but unpopular models go begging. Insurance on an older model also costs less.

Again, your trusty mechanic may be your best resource and may know a customer with a perfectly adequate car who wants to trade it in for one reason or another: a bigger family, a smaller family, the new-car-every-three-years syndrome, whatever. Your mechanic will also know that car's condition and your needs. Even if the mechanic has no sellers to suggest, ask for specific recommendations that you can look for. Mechanics know lemons to avoid. (Also check such magazines as *Consumer Reports* for statistics and ratings on frequency of repair for various car models.) Lastly, ask the mechanic the cost—and most convenient time for—a once-over inspection of any car you consider. The nominal cost, if you don't have too many finalists, is worth it.

When you're ready for the actual hunt, check these places: newspaper classifieds, grocery bulletin boards, neighbors, relatives, friends, church bulletin boards, company newsletters, car rental companies, fleet owners (such as insurance or computer companies), new car dealers. Don't be beguiled by low mileage; those miles may have been extremely hard ones. You can eliminate a lot of cars by a simple glance or a fifteen-minute ride.

Have the tires worn unevenly? Are the fenders or under-door panels rusty? Is there rust under the rugs? Are there obvious leaks underneath? Is there a front-end shimmy, a swerve when you brake, an excessively loose steering wheel, a noisy rear end, a smoky or noisy exhaust, a choppy motor? Has there obviously been an accident in its history? If it looks and sounds okay or even "not too bad," take it to your mechanic who should check the "heavy" stuff, including engine compression, brakes, ball joints, chassis, and shocks. You might even talk over the asking price with your mechanic. If the opinion is affirmative, you may just have found yourself a gem.

Once you have this jewel, treasure it through regular, loving care. Meantime, make every penny count. My natural inclination is to advise you to get a bike. Or walk. Preserve that car as long as you can, save some money, and keep your body in shape all at the same time. But most of us place great reliance on our automobiles, so my advice must be to get every mile you can from each gallon of gas. Observe these few simple cautions and you'll find your fill-ups less frequent.

Don't pump the throttle when you start up. A single push is all you need. Even a few extra pumps on cold starts (cold engine, not necessarily cold days) quickly accumulate to gallons wasted.

Let the engine idle rather fast for no more than thirty seconds, then start off slowly.

After the engine has warmed, go into top gear as soon as feasible (you don't want bucking). Lower gears require more fuel.

Try not to downshift any more than necessary. Same reason—wasted fuel.

Don't coast on downhills (dangerous), but do remember to on lesser grades such as parking lots and city blocks.

Drive as smoothly as possible, but let your car slow if you must climb a steep grade.

Take plenty of time when you pass another car, avoiding excessive gear changes or throttle settings.

Don't drive with your foot on the brake.

"Look at that leg!" my husband exclaimed. His tone was one of admiration. But the leg he was looking at was not mine. It was his own. There was not a bit of "jiggle" to it. Commuting to work by bicycle pares flab as well as transportation costs.

For Jack, round trip by bus costs $3.20 per day. That's $64 per month, assuming twenty working days. Subtract three rain days, and we still save $55 per month when Jack rides his bike. He can't ride year round, maybe seven months out of twelve, but I'll not sniff at $385.

Even more marked is the contrast to driving by car. Parking alone costs at least $80 per month. (Who says the living's not expensive here in the nation's capital?) Add to that fuel, car maintenance, and extra insurance commuters must pay. The monthly total easily approaches $125. Car-pooling with one or two others drops that to $62 or $41 per person. Compare that to pedal power!

Not that bicycling is totally free. We spend $50 per year for servicing and new parts. And underwear. Nine miles, even on a cool morning, can rot your socks faster than you'd believe possible. Jack changes at the office, which means either twice as much underwear or twice as many (though smaller) laundry loads. Since I do both the shopping and the laundry, I chose new underwear. And the cost of his bike, a five-speed Peugeot? Well under fifty dollars, secondhand.

Jack's nine-mile trek takes an hour, about twenty minutes more than the bus trip. Most of his route follows a recognized bike path where the only danger is the occasional two-wheeled hot-rodder. Take advantage of a bike path, even if it lengthens your trip. Should a bike path not be available, work out your route in advance. A local bike club may have already mapped the safest routes, developed from experience.

Cycle carefully to avoid accidents. Your chances of being hit from the rear are slight. You're more likely to find yourself in trouble at intersections, especially when you turn corners. Keep a careful eye out for parked motorists who swing car doors open suddenly. Act like a vehicle: flow with the traffic, obey traffic signals, use signals to tell traffic what you're doing. You'll have a better idea of what you're doing if you wear a rearview mirror, a little one on your wrist or clipped to your eyeglasses or helmet. A helmet should be standard equipment if you travel in traffic. And if you ride at dawn or dusk, make sure you have good lights and reflectors.

8

Twenty-one Nights on the QE2? Who Needs It!

*It is not good to have zeal
without knowledge,
nor to be hasty and miss
the way.*

PROVERBS 19:2

Come summertime and vacation chatter, the line that drives me crazy is not "I thought I'd *finally* get a full month of that glorious Greek sun (last summer we had *only* two weeks, remember?), but my husband *insists* we take the last weekend to cool off—in Copenhagen." The one that gets me goes something like this: "We've decided that the only way to get some relaxation is to pull out the barbecue and enjoy our own backyard this year." It leaves me speechless. To reply, "That sounds *wonderful!*" or "Have a great time." may be the polite response, but coming from me they're unnatural. I try not to say, "Oh, that's too bad." I pity their lack of money, but even more, I pity their lack of imagination.

Vacation is spelled t-r-a-v-e-l, to me. (Anyone who knows me knows my itchy feet.) So where does that leave us in a year when the slightest swerve in the budget would blow it all to bits? Do I revise my definitions? My husband would advise you not to ask! Let's just say I *refined* my definitions. . . .

We bought bikes. Jack and the baby on one, JC and myself on another, off we pedaled. One could not say we exactly covered the continent, but we did go a long way in discovering what family recreation is all about.

But, you say, for what a bicycle costs today, you can pay for a lot of motel time, an airplane seat or two. True. We almost did.

I had been requested to do a chapter on bikes for a consumer buying-guide. I researched bikes exhaustively, became the ultimate savvy shopper. By the time I finished writing the chapter, I was convinced (still am!) of my own advice: bikes are the only way to go.

Bikes were a good idea, my husband allowed. He, too, was compelled by the exuberance of color and youth that whizzed past us daily as we trudged along on our sedate family strolls. Even the white-haired riders on their whirling flashes of blue or green or yellow appeared younger than we felt, watching them. Exercise. Fresh air. Fun. We needed them all. But first we needed bikes.

The first shop was a disaster. Biking may retain its laid-back reputation, but the marketing of it has not. The shop was so crammed with paraphernalia, evidently successfully enticing Saturday-morning swarms of zealous cyclists, that we had to *search* for the bikes. Then we had to *ask* for prices (there were no tags). The lifted eyebrows of the clerk made it clear we were not typical clientele. We tried to make our exit casual.

"Well!" I said on our way to the car. "I know of another shop." I tried to sound upbeat. After all, this was supposed to be my bailiwick.

I sighed with relief as we pulled up to the second shop. Children whizzed up and down the sidewalk out front, trying out models with names I recognized. Inside, clustered near the doorway, were the trade-ins, with brand name, wheel size, frame size—and price!—carefully noted. I ignored them as I smiled triumphantly at Jack and motioned him toward a chair in the corner.

"This should take no time at all," I assured him. I turned toward the *new* bikes. It was just a matter of fit. Any model would do, as far as price was concerned. They seemed so cheap. They weren't really, of course. The prices were merely reasonable, cheap only in comparison to the outrageous prices of the first shop. And, I finally had to admit, they were still beyond our means.

I glanced at Jack, patiently entertaining Alexis in the corner. "Which do you like better?" I mouthed at him, pointing toward two, my smile becoming brittle again. He walked over.

"Are you sure you can afford that?" He did not yet realize my intention to buy *two*, one to replace the rusty but usable bike neither of us had ridden in years. "Remember, we have to get a seat for Alexis —who, by the way, needs a clean diaper."

I hated the picture: financially struggling suburbanites bickering over what should seem like a few dollars. Sure, the other bikes had been out of the question. But these too? I wanted to be somebody's bratty twelve-year-old, click-click-clicking the gears as I pulled away on yet another two-hundred-dollar gesture of affection from an ever-indulgent daddy. No checkbook to balance, no diapers to change.

"Let's call it a day," I sighed. "We'll check the classifieds tomorrow." I tried to keep the resentment out of my eyes as I looked at somebody's pigtailed daughter, about twelve, disentangling from its pile a bike I'd been considering. I turned to follow Jack and the girls.

The man at the door had just wheeled in a Peugeot and a Raleigh and was examining the price tags of the other used bikes. "We're going to trade them in on new ones," he explained, nodding his head first toward his bikes and then toward the pigtails. "She and her sister have been saving their baby-sitting money for two years, and their mother and I are going to throw in whatever we can get for these two we picked up secondhand in Europe a couple years ago." Fondly he patted the Peugeot's saddle. "What do you think they're worth?"

Sure (and almost hoping) he wouldn't take it, I made an offer of thirty dollars. He paused. "Let me talk to the clerk," he finally said. I tried not to hover too near. How much would the shop offer? My excitement was growing. "Thirty-five," he came back to say.

So the Raleigh became mine. A check to him, another to the shop mechanic for a tune-up, a tire, a car rack, plus the best quality child's seat money can buy: Our total was still under a hundred dollars! We went back later and bought the Peugeot for Jack. Our total expenditure for bikes and equipment was under $175—not even a third of what I had *almost* spent.

We might have found equally good deals through lawn sales or classifieds or at a police auction. Bike shops have their disadvantages, primarily the higher prices. Jack's Peugeot, for instance, would have cost less if we had snatched it up at the time we bought my Raleigh from the man who came to make a trade-in. But classifieds can be tricky. Anyone who knows enough to publish wheel size, frame size, and other relevant information a wise shopper looks for is likely to know enough to get top dollar. Anyone who goes to the bother of advertising will want more than someone who, at the last minute, decides to drag it out to the lawn with other clutter they want to be rid of. Tracking down such a bargain can mean indefinite delay. Even then it might not fit or might be in irreparable condition.

Bike shops accept only bikes they know are saleable, those with remediable problems. They can make a bike road-ready and safe so that it doesn't become just another irritant waiting for your own garage sale. Shop mechanics can send you off on a bike that fits.

Sometimes this is just a simple matter of adjustment: changing the seat, raising or adjusting the handlebars, or merely tightening a bolt. These are things you'd probably have to have done to your auction or lawn-sale bike, anyway. The chances of happening on a perfect fit that's perfectly tuned are slim. But without such a bike you'll be uncomfortable and quickly become frustrated (to say nothing of being unsafe).

Wheel size on adult bikes is no problem. There are just two: twenty-six and twenty-seven inch. **Frame** size—seventeen to twenty-six inches—is more complicated. If you're trying out a man's frame, you should be able to feel an inch or so between your crotch and the frame tube. If you have a woman's model, measure your inseam length to the floor and subtract nine inches. This is your correct frame size (the distance from the crank axle to the top frame tube). A mixte frame (like a woman's but with an extra, sloping cross tube) is measured the same way. Better to err on the small size; too large a frame is not under the rider's control. Also, be sure the frame is strong—no welds.

Many serious bikers advise everyone to buy "diamond" (their jargon for the man's frame) and to go with at least a ten-speed. I don't agree. The diamond may be lighter and stronger and appropriate to most readers (including myself, someday), but not to someone who's toting weight in back and must dismount fast and often. Toting a child, I want total control every second. I do agree, though, that the bike should be **lightweight.** Every extra pound makes a difference when you're straining on that uphill. Skip the fenders.

The plaudits given ten-speeds are sometimes unjustified. What matters is the **gear ratio,** roughly described as the difference in how hard you have to pedal in your lowest speed compared to your highest speed. Some ten-speeds have a wide ratio—lots of difference—but others do not. The same is true of various three- or five-speed models. What you're after in any bike is uphill climb that requires as little strain as possible plus a pleasant ride in top speed. How fast that is depends on what you want and need. The nuances inbetween, on a ten-speed, are just that; they also mean trickier maintenance and repairs.

Handlebars and saddles (seats) are another controversial subject, not as important as frame or speeds. My opinion wavers. When I'm on my own —no burden in back to hold me down or make me nervous about balance—I like dropped handlebars so I can "let it out." Once you become accustomed to them, they are unarguably more comfortable and better for your back than the old-fashioned, touring, upright style. But with a child it's hardly "life in the fast lane." And if it's not a child, it's a bag of groceries. So I have the old uprights. Whichever style you choose, make sure the handlebars are adjusted to a height that's comfortable, probably the same level as the front of the saddle.

I also use a cushioned vinyl seat. That's *only* because I can't afford leather, infinitely more comfortable—*after* it's broken in, which takes a season! By all means, avoid the old-fashioned hammer seat and adjust the one of your choice to a position where, sitting on the saddle and resting the ball of your foot on a pedal at its lowest position, you have only a slight bend at the knee. Make sure that both the seat post and the handlebar stem extend at least two inches into the frame tubes.

That **brakes** should be trustworthy goes without saying. If they shudder or squeal or if you can squeeze them all the way to the handlebars, they need adjusting! Again, there is a discussion as to best kind: center-pull or side-pull. Side-pulls have fewer moving parts and are simpler to adjust. High-quality side-pulls cost more than high-quality center-pulls. Since the alternative is a low-quality side-pull, go with center-pulls. Avoid the brake extension levers which allow you to brake from the top of the handlebars; they aren't reliable for quick stops. Neither are coaster (foot) brakes.

Any secondhand bike is likely to need new tires. Do not assume that wider is better. Let a shop mechanic advise you on proper tires. Next time you can shop for the same tire for less money at a large toy or discount store, but it does no good to shop without knowing what you need. The same bike mechanic can make your bike road-ready. Some shops offer a limited guarantee on bikes you buy from them, even secondhand ones. Until you've become familiar with your bike's mechanism, the mechanic is also the one to install lights, brakes, and chains. Child seats should always be installed by a reputable mechanic.

Bikes being big business these days, **bike books** abound. They are not all equal, although they tend to overlap or duplicate. The popular classic (and for good reason) is *Anybody's Bike Book* by Tom Cuthbertson ($4.95 from Ten Speed Press, Box 7123, Berkeley, California 94707). It tells, without being long-winded as many bike texts are, how to choose, maintain, repair, and enjoy a bike. You do not have to be either the owner of a six-hundred dollar import or a Saturday mechanic to appreciate this book, which you can find at most bike shops. A book you may have to write for, also by Cuthbertson and his illustrator, Rick Morall, is *The Bike Bag Book* ($2.95 from Ten Speed Press), aptly subtitled "a manual for emergency roadside bicycle repair," one of two pieces of paraphernalia I wouldn't wheel out without (even though I'm not a mechanic). The other is a tiny rearview mirror that attaches to my glasses. These cost about five dollars.

Now that you're all equipped, **where do you go?** Around the block, for starters. We almost killed ourselves getting out of our alley the first time. Balance, with a child in back, is completely different, sometimes impossible. As is gearing. As is braking. Pebbles and potholes I sail right over, by myself, become obstacles when I tote extra weight. Riding a bike may be one of those skills that, once learned, you never forget, but you need to acquaint yourself with the quirks of your "new" two-wheeler, your "new" circumstances. Don't forget to inquire about local ordinances. Some jurisdictions want you to ride *with* car traffic, others *against* it. Some want you on the sidewalk, others on the road.

Now you're ready to explore the local park from a two-wheeled perspective. We've spent many a pleasant Sunday afternoon lollygagging around ours. A loaf of bread, a hunk of cheese, and some fruit: I wouldn't trade the repose for a week of bustle in some alien city. A word of caution: always carry some beverage. Camping and outdoor stores sell featherweight plastic containers you can fill the night before and freeze. The bandits of the bike trails are the lemonade kids. Remember when it was a penny a cup? Remember Jacob and Esau? Any more than a few miles on your first ride, and you'll be *glad* to ante up the quarter a swallow the urchins are demanding these days.

Once you've gained a little confidence (read: leg muscle), you're ready to accumulate some mileage on the bike trails. When I was a child, my cousin and I had a plan to design bike routes stretching hither, thither, and yon—every place a car could go. We even sent a letter suggesting this to the president. Somehow the word must have filtered through, because today there are bike trails almost everywhere. Finding them is the problem. Once you do, you can latch on to one for as few or as many miles as you like. Some are as short as two or three miles. Then there's the TransAmerica Trail! Yes, many of them are loop trails so you needn't retrace your route, although I've never seen a road that didn't look at least a little bit different when viewed from the opposite direction. Some are back roads. Others are paved paths reserved for cyclists. Some are a combination. Many wend right through suburbia and center city, but most try to avoid high traffic areas—*car* traffic! Apparently it's not been resolved who has the right of way on bike paths—joggers or bikers.

Those of us more casual and less experienced than the cross-country zealots have them to thank for making our search for routes much easier. They have compiled trail guides and maps ("tours," they're often called, but not to be confused with "guided tours"). Unfortunately, there's no comprehensive list of these tours; there's not even a comprehensive list of lists. But a few conscientious groups are doing their best to keep up with the rapid growth of the network of trails. Here are some of these groups and the resources they offer.

About the best is Bikecentennial. The founders of this organization must be the ones who got wind of my plea to the president. This is the group we heard so much about in 1976 when four thousand of them celebrated the Bicentennial with a coast-to-coast ride. Since then, they've developed and mapped a network of routes in addition to their inspiration for 1976, the TransAmerica Trail. Much of

Bikecentennial's effort is geared (no pun intended) toward the beginning cyclist. In *The Cyclists' Yellow Pages*, updated annually, they pinpoint state and local sources, public and private, that give information helpful to cyclists. Some of this material Bikecentennial keeps on file; you can order it directly from them. The *Yellow Pages* are $2.50, free if you join. When you write, ask for *Bikecentennial Bookstore* (a free catalog of some two hundred titles) and mention that you're a novice and would appreciate all the free help you can get. This group is not so big that they don't give individual attention. A real homespun organization, they may send you quite a bit. For sure you'll get a membership solicitation, which may or may not interest you. (Write: Bikecentennial, P.O. Box 8308, Missoula, Montana 59807.)

Another organization is AYH, or American Youth Hostels. It, too, is a membership organization that serves nonmembers. (A little note. One thing I've noticed about these bike/recreation groups: They are not greedy. They encourage one another, even defer to one another in their zest for their shared goal of promoting bicycling, and the proper facilities for it, nationwide. They often duplicate services, but they *always* include their "competition" in their recommendations.) The free catalog from AYH is titled *AYH's Discount Storeroom*. The AYH parallel of Bikecentennial's *Yellow Pages* is *The American Bicycle Atlas,* for $6.95. AYH now bills itself as "the up and coming low-cost travel organization"—more about that on pages 144–45. (Write: AYH, 1332 I St. NW, Washington, D.C. 20005.)

• • •

The information available from and through bike groups is good for anyone to whom money is an object. Cyclists tend not to be high-budget travelers. Nor do they frequent fast-food eateries or the predictable hotel chains. Sights, lodgings, eats mentioned in publications you buy from Bikecentennial or AYH tend to be low-cost and offbeat. You may recognize some of the books in their catalogs if you've already scouted out offbeat, low-cost lodgings.

There are cheap lodgings, and then there are lodgings that are CHEAP! Topping the list of the second category are "hospitality homes." You can't find anything cheaper than these. Some are free. There are two similar listings and a third that is truly unique.

The Touring Cyclists' Hospitality Directory is a listing of some one thousand homes (maybe barns or backyards) where travelers *arriving by bike* can stay for free. The catch: the directory is available only to people who agree to let their own names be listed! Listing your name does not mean you must surrender your own bed to a different stranger every night. Travelers make arrangements in advance. If you've had more than your share, of course, you can explain this. (Write: John Mosley, 13623 Sylvan, Van Nuys, California 91401.) Oh, yes! A shower's included!

A similar listing is maintained by LAW, the League of American Wheelmen, a national organization more than one hundred years old. LAW volunteers agree to open their homes, for free, to other LAW members who need not agree to reciprocate. A side benefit of joining LAW is the benefit of "touring information directors' in each state, a virtually free travel agency that specializes in biking." (Write: League of American Wheelmen (LAW), 10

East Read St., P.O. Box 988, Baltimore, Maryland 21203.)

A third hospitality system (not "for bikers only") is quite different in purpose and design. For Christians who like to make new friends through fellowship, it may be the best resource of the three. There is only one caveat, and that is a major one: this listing is ONLY for those travelers who are interested in fellowship as well as a place to stay. It is not a "sleep and run" arrangement, although one-night stays are the usual. Traveling this way takes more time. Thrift was secondary in the minds of Leon and Nancy Stauffer when they started the *Mennonite-Your-Way Directory*. A network of new friends for Christian fellowship was the primary reason, evident in the thoroughness of the directory's listings. Each is coded not only for such practicalities as "space for camper," "playpen available," but for interests, occupation, age of children, and church affiliation. Guests contact the host directly *at least* two weeks in advance. A contribution of three to five dollars is usually left with the host family. More is given if the guest accepts the offer of a meal—*not* part of the deal. The latest listing of some two thousand names, to which you need not add your own, costs under ten dollars. (Write: Leon and Nancy Stauffer, Box 1525, Salunga, Pennsylvania 17538.)

Hostels are a thrifty, often overlooked, form of accommodation. There are more than three hundred hostels nationwide, city and country. Unlike what you may have heard (because of a few European examples), a hostel bed is *not* a group bunk! It may be hard, it may be lumpy, it's likely to be dormitory style, but you get it all to yourself. The price may make it more attractive. Hostels average $4.50 per night per person, and you can stay up to three consecutive nights. A family pass reduces the rate, except in extremely popular hostels. Sometimes there are special facilities for families. Sleeping bags are not encouraged, so you save yourself the bother of something extra in your back seat or on your bike. Your bike, should you arrive that way, will get you a nod of approval. It's considered a "hosteling activity" (along with hiking, canoeing, visiting historic monuments, etc.) in which anyone arriving by "motorized transportation," as they so quaintly phrase it, is expected to participate. You need a membership to use AYH accommodations, which are listed in the *Handbook of Youth Hostels*. The handbook is updated annually and priced at $2.50 for non-members. Members get it free.

Besides price, there are other aspects of hosteling which make it attractive. It's wholesome. The basic premise of the organization is—leave a place better than you find it. You may be asked to sweep a floor or perform some other simple chore. Alcohol and drugs are not permitted, and smoking is allowed only in designated areas. Usually there's a fully equipped kitchen where you can make your own meals. The showers are *usually* hot. Some hostels are in cities, but mostly they are on or near hiking and biking trails or in scenic, historic, or recreational areas. This explains why you see so many bikes and backpacks at them. Membership is open to anyone. A family membership costs twenty-one dollars per year, but there are other types. All run December through December unless you join in the last three months of the year, meaning you *can* get fifteen months for the price of twelve. Write the AYH address, given a few paragraphs above, or call (toll free) 800-424-9426. (When money is less of an issue, you can take advantage of AYH-sponsored charter flights.)

MORE LODGING

College campuses are an inexpensive lodging during the summertime ($6–$16 in 1982), when many schools open up empty dorms. (But watch out for "learning vacations" many colleges and universities offer: a great idea on a regular budget; not so smart if you're on a tight one.) Some schools which rent dorm beds let you take advantage of the cafeteria and sports facilities. Some require you to bring your own bedding, but others don't allow it. Most require reservations, and a few stipulate that you must be an educator or alumnus. For current information on the whole kit and caboodle of them, world-wide, get a copy of *U.S. and Worldwide Travel Accommodations Guide,* for $4.95 (Teachers Tax Service, 1303 E. Balboa Blvd., Newport Beach, California 92661).

Elderhostels are a super idea if you and (or) your spouse are over sixty, and if you each have $150 per week to spend on a vacation, not including transportation. That's what it takes to get you five nights (Sunday through Friday), three squares a day, and as many as fifteen classes (three per day, Monday through Friday). You can study (but not for credit) anything from anthropology to computers to poetry to zoology. And no one will tell if you play hooky. About six hundred colleges and universities offer Elderhostel educational vacations, many of them so popular that "students" must sign on by March or postpone their first or second choices until the next season. All the Elderhostel programs are operated in basically the same way, but where you go depends on what your transportation budget allows as well as what you want to study; not all schools offer the same courses, and many of them are designed around local special environmental, cultural, or historical features. Catalogs and registration forms are mailed in January, but the people who run the program adivse you to get your name on the mailing list well before then. (Write: Elderhostel, 100 Boylston Street, Suite 200, Boston, Massachusetts 02116.

Bed and breakfasts (B & Bs) will be to the 1980s what fast-food franchises were to the 1960s. They are revolutionizing the lodging industry, and they are going to do to the price of a bed what McDonald's did to the hamburger. But B & Bs increase variety rather than destroy it. No two homes have spare bedrooms exactly alike, and that's what B & Bs are— spare bedrooms and a clean (but not necessarily separate) bath shared with paying guests who stay for breakfast. They're on farms, in cities and small towns, off the beaten track, and in the center of things. Most don't hang a shingle, so you must hunt them out. There are several local and regional referral agencies as well as a few directories which can help you. Nearly two dozen of the referral agencies are contained in *Bed & Breakfast U.S.A.: A Guide to Guest Houses and Tourist Homes* by Betty Rundback and Nancy Ackerman ($5.95 from E.P. Dutton or write to the authors at RD 2, Box 355A, Greentown, Pennsylvania 18426). When Rundback compiled her first annual guide a few years ago, she had barely a few dozen homes to list; the 1982 edition gives you access to more than 2,000 places, so popular have B & Bs become. Another, newer directory is *BABS* (Bed and Breakfast Service) by Delores and George Herrmann, who started their service many years ago but only recently began publishing a directory. So they, too, are old hands in this business. The Herrmann directory, updated in November, is considerably smaller (for the moment only, I have no doubt) and costs $2.75 (Write directly to the Herrmanns, *BABS*, Box 5025, Bellingham,

Washington 98227.) Like the Rundback directory, the Herrmann directory covers the entire nation and includes referral services; but unlike it, addresses for individual homes are not listed, only telephone numbers. ("We think the American public is not ready to take folks off the street"—an understandable conclusion.) The Herrmanns screen all hosts they list; they require a picture of the home and room and try to visit it.

Referral agencies also try to exert quality control. As well as screening housing facilities periodically, they try to match "personalities" of host and guest. Their commission comes from the host. All directories and agencies should provide information on pets, parking, facilities for children, etc. (information also contained in the Rundback and Herrmann guides).

B & Bs are not the cheapest way to go (prices vary radically), but they're certainly one of the most pleasant, as anyone who's traveled in the British Isles—where they've been popular for years—can attest. Not that you can expect a private telephone or a four-course breakfast served in bed; usually the breakfast is Continental—coffee or tea, juice, a sweet roll or doughnut. Just like home. Well, almost.

GROUP VACATIONS

Here's a great way to splurge on a trip you might not otherwise be able to afford. Every Labor Day weekend for the past six years, we and several friends have shared a log cabin deep in a West Virginia forest. Some years there are as few as six of us to split the costs. Sometimes we are as many as a dozen (those years we rent two cabins side by side.) Ours is no hot dog and beans weekend. We dine on Fettucini Alfredo (parmesan grated fresh on the spot, of course) and the like despite our habitat, which offers none of the kitchen conveniences of home. No electricity, just softly purring gas chandeliers and an antiquated woodburning stove with a filthy flue. No running water, just a creaking pump out back and a trout stream out front. It's grand, it's isolated, and it's only about $25 per adult. Of course, it takes five hours of switchback mountain curves to get there.

After all these years, we've worked out a planning system you can adapt. Way back in February somebody has to call the ranger to find out the new price (we take advantage of the all-but-unknown toll-free telephone number), then collect a deposit from anyone who wants to go. The amount is determined by number of people and by current price of the cabin and by whether we reserve it just for the weekend or for the whole week. (If we don't go, we lose our deposit—unless we find a sub acceptable to all the others.) We make our reservation by early March. Remote though they may be, these cabins go early.

About mid-August we get together for a planning party, itself something of a joint effort. Everybody brings something. Our August reunion sort of gets us in the mood; we become reacquainted and figure our logistics. Whoever goes first picks up the key and bedding at the ranger's—no small task, we discovered the first year. We arrived after midnight and learned that the ranger's cabin is (unless you drive a four-wheel-drive) an hour's drive each way. Those who go before Friday not only pick up the key but make their own food arrangements.

Planned menus begin with Friday night. From then on, menus are accounted for; if you say you'll be there, you're figured into the purchase order and, thus, charged for the meal when the weekend is over.

We serve only two meals per day: a brunch that would put most buffets to shame and a late (between 10:10 P.M. and midnight) dinner. Snacks are a big part of the grocery bill. Each person solos or is part of a two-person team for one or two meals, depending how big the crowd and how expansive the menu. The person who cooks buys the groceries for that meal (the menu has already been agreed on by all at the planning meeting). One person buys all the snacks according to preferences and estimates given at the meeting. This avoids expensive, unpopular duplicates but assures there will be enough. You think such detail unnecessary? One year we emptied our sixth box of Wheat Thins within twenty-four hours of our arrival. Despite the fact that we had three grocery bags of similar snacks, we sent someone for more this hands-down favorite. The nearest store being a miserable hour of logging road away, it took that long to decide who must go. But there was no doubt one of us would! The only other chore for which volunteers are reluctant is the dish detail. All us city slickers, of course, love to chop wood and pump water.

One thing we've learned is to carry supplies that the cabin is supposed to have in stock: wicks for the gas lamps, waterproof matches (lots!), dish cloths, detergent, toilet paper. And after the first year, everyone has brought a can of air spray for the outhouse. Another thing for which such cabins are notorious is refrigerators: they're small and ill-behaved. Take your own ice and plan your menus so that food won't perish.

The day we leave the forest, everyone gives their shopping receipts to one person who does the math either there or on the way home. By then we're all a little frayed and in a rush to clean the cabin, so no one wants to worry about who owes whom exactly how much so that everything comes out to the penny. We try to make everybody happy within a week.

And that's the weekend. By the way, you're probably wondering why we eat such late dinners. Because we nap like hibernating bears in the afternoons (exhausted from our hikes as much as overstuffed from our sumptuous brunches) and begin prolonged games about the time normal people begin dinner preparations. I can't remember any activity—not even sleep—in which everybody participated simultaneously, except for meals. Nobody wants the bother of being boss. That's why the weekends work; we've planned them well enough so nobody feels they must assume responsibility.

EXCHANGING HOUSES

If you don't want to share your vacation time with a group, consider this plan. We have country friends who occasionally exchange houses with some of their city friends. Both families get the advantage of no-cost lodging and at-home meal prices. They have, I presume, worked out the details on bedding and keys, woodpiles and pets, and every other likely disaster that might endanger a friendship. You can work out a similar deal with your own friends, or you can stay at a stranger's place you locate through a house exchange network. Check page 68 for the addresses of a few of these exchange services. They aren't free, but they're sure less than a hotel bill.

FREEBIES

Wherever you go, there are free things to see and do. Don't overlook them. Some interesting places (How about touring a chocolate factory?) welcome but don't solicit. A couple of directories (not free) have compiled lists of free things (primarily tourist sights such as monuments and parks), but for broader and better information go through the state and local travel bureaus of the places you plan to visit. You can find the addresses (and sometimes toll-free telephone numbers) through various sources available from AYH and Bikecentennial, mentioned earlier in this chapter.

Lots of interesting freebies are mentioned in the *Harvard Let's Go—the Budget Guide to the U.S.A.* (St. Martin's Press). This book is exactly what you might expect: travel information for and by students on a typically low student budget, to everywhere a student might go. Everything is represented: transportation (intra as well as inter-city), food, lodging, entertainment, tourist sights, local history and lore. Don't expect a compendium of *all* the information from *all* the other travel books—just a more-than-adequate cross section. As the saying goes, "If you can buy only one book, this is it." The European edition guided my husband and I around Europe on $3 per person per day (of course, that was in 1974), And, yes, I would do it again, if my choices were another four-month European vacation in similar style or none at all. *Let's Go* is completely revised each year, so buy it in the spring.

A WORD ABOUT WINTER. . . .

All this advice is fine, I hear you say, but summer is but a single season. What about the rest of the year?

Most of the accommodations mentioned in this chapter are available year-round. You may find them to be cheaper in the off-season, usually the winter. But about bikes: they're usable for at *least* six months of the year. In many places you can stretch that six months to eight or nine. A good deal of the three or four remaining are generally so miserable that I recommend drawing the curtains and curling up with a good book. Better yet, buy trilogies; the stories drag on till the drifts disappear. Refinish furniture. Improve your chess. Bake some cookies. (Console yourself with enough of them, and you'll need to get out on that bike, come the first balmy days of spring.) That is not vacation time, anyway—when the days are short and the icicles long. It may be time for a get-away by some desperate folk, but don't confuse that ephemeral desire for a holiday with the genuine need for a summer vacation.

Some people spend great amounts of money on ski vacations and call them a bargain because they managed a group rate on lodgings and lift tickets. A long-time skier myself (I grew up in the New York Adirondacks where there's snow from late November through April), I know it takes a lot of hours coming downhill to make the dollars spent getting up there pass for any kind of bargain. I admit I've never skied cross-country. If I were to return to snow country, I would have advice to offer on places and equipment. Here in Virginia the nearest snow, except for a week or two, is at least an hour away. But let me tell you about the ice skates I found for a dollar. . . .

9

Did the Magi Have A Charge Account?

Better a dry crust with peace and quiet than a house full of feasting, with strife.

PROVERBS 17:1

Christmas is a heady time. Witness, for most of us, the bills that roll in afterward, about the same time as the tax forms. Last year, panicky at the thought of the pauper's Christmas that lay ahead on "half our income," I went for broke. I bought my child every gift she might conceivably desire for several Christmases hence, however inappropriate to her four-year-old interests. And I bought the best: Madame Alexander dolls, Stieff stuffed animals, Italian paints. My pen never paused when the sales clerk at the doll store asked in horror, "You're not buying these for her to *play* with, are you?" I most certainly was, my eyes informed her as I, with a flourish, signed yet another credit card receipt. Not only that, I wanted several custom-made doll accessories, too.

It wasn't that I shopped with abandon. It was with forethought. It seemed the sensible thing to do. She'd never have another Christmas as an only child, was my reasoning. I wanted to give her one to remember. And I wanted to give her the best—so it would last. (It was probably also "one last fling" for mother.)

My thinking was completely backward. Who appreciates what they have until they've had a time without? More to the point, what four-year-old cares what her doll will be worth when she reaches the incomprehensible age of thirty?

Now, a year later, several months after that then-dreaded Christmas, the $40-doll is stashed deep in my daughter's closet. It lay untouched for several months while she played with the trendy $4.98 Strawberry Shortcake and Blueberry Muffin dolls I bought in reluctant acquiescence to her wishes. And the easel—a half-price bargain my consumerist antennae would not let slip away—stands nearly as immaculate as it was last December 25. Meantime, she paints and draws wherever she can clear a space in whatever room I occupy.

This is not to say quality doesn't count. Yes, the Alexander doll (twice removed from the closet's recesses) has hair that could respond with amazing forbearance to a five-year-old cosmetician. Yes, by the time that five-year-old has a daughter of her own the doll will have appreciated in monetary value. But what if, as was the fate of poor Blueberry, that cosmetician decides that shorter is better and puts a scissors to those lovely locks? It won't be doll or daughter who suffers. It will be mother. My investment will be ruined. Far better to have "saved" money by putting it away for another Christmas, even this one when the bounty of last year led my daughter to—by Halloween—quite innocently put three dolls on her Santa list.

So what does Santa do? Let me tell you about this Christmas.

I'd like to relate some heartwarming, two-hankie tale, but old habits don't die that easily. Our holiday spending still exceeded the tight budget we'd established as an aim. But that budget was less than half what we'd spent the Christmas prior, and in our post-holiday analysis we realized how slight was the excess. In one way we could even congratulate ourselves. True, we'd overshot the dollar figure we'd set informally; that failure we had to admit. But neither of us had approached the *real* maximum we had each secretly established but not divulged to each other until after Christmas. Other than that our Christmas was unqualifiedly a financial success. It took no little planning and some painful self-restraint—at first. By the end of the season, however, it was easier to keep the wallet tucked away than to pull it out. Afterward was even better! There were few credit card bills to pay, and I had a headful of ways to cut next Christmas's expenses by half again, making this upcoming holiday one-quarter as expensive as the one a mere two seasons ago.

Our holiday was as merry as ever. We gave as many gifts and (I like to think) better ones than last year; they weren't extravagant bric-a-brac. We had more cookies than were good for us, but not so many that we were still eating them way into Lent. We entertained as much, but not with a series of expensive, five-course dinners for eight. We had as many gifts under the tree, but none that weren't in use by New Year's.

But I said old habits die hard. There were a couple of bills to pay, even if they were small, and there was a Stieff leopard under the tree. Am I rationalizing when I say it was the one gift we gave to the ten-month-old (who had eyes only for wrappings and ribbons) and we found it on a 30-percent-off sale, as unprecedented for Stieff animals as snowmen in July? (A child has only one "first Christmas" after all!) The leopard was really the only indulgence, if you don't count the butter. Unsalted butter goes for $2.27 per pound in our town, at least during the holiday months when my kitchen won't settle for less.

Christmas cookies, which is where the butter went, may be the best symbol of this year's different kind of Christmas. Cookies have always been a major part of Christmas, since way before the time I realized cookbook authors and myself might have differing definitions as to what constituted "good" in a cookie. Some of my most treasured childhood memories are of sitting at the kitchen table with my mother on blustery, gray December afternoons, spreading colored glop into intricate designs only a mother—and a six-year-old—could appreciate, could recognize! Nothing I've made since has been so perfect.

But I go into an annual frenzy trying to find satisfactory substitutes. Usually we're still chewing on stars, bells, and topless trees when neighbors are ready to bring out the Valentine hearts. That's a lot of butter! This year we licked our fingers appreciatively for the last time on New Year's. Everyone had had their fill but could still cinch the belt buckle. We had cut the butter consumption, still the cost equivalent of a week's groceries, by half, as well as the chocolate, sugar, raisins, nuts, and other ingredients that can double that figure again. Nuts and raisins I don't mind buying. As a matter of fact, the money I saved on this year's drop in butter I invested in nuts for the freezer. Walnuts are pure protein for $2.49 per pound, and it doesn't add a penny to the utility bill to put them on the table, unlike more usual protein sources such as meat and eggs. I saved more dollars by comparison shopping for holiday baking ingredients. The next best price on walnuts, for example, was fifty cents more per pound.

Something else I did this Christmas (it's so simple I can't believe I learned it at thirty years of age!) was learn to make colored sugars for Christmas cookies. Approval of food dyes is not the norm for me; Christmas is the exception. Nor do I like the idea of paying sixty-three cents for three ounces of colored sugar. JC's the only one in the family who even likes the look of colored sugar on cookies. Now I can make her happy at least once a year by putting her on this little project.

> Find several jars (one for each color you want) with tight lids. Put in a cup of sugar, add ¼ teaspoon of water and a drop or two of liquid food coloring. (To get bright red, use the paste red available from most fancy food stores.) Shake each jar to mix the contents. Then, one color at a time, spread on a cookie sheet and dry in a warm oven for about five minutes. Mash the sugar until it's as fine as you want it and put it back into its storage container.

Speaking of butter and sugar and mouth-directed indulgences, may I diverge momentarily? There is one cookie, unknown in my childhood, but which is now as indispensable to my family's Christmas as I assume plum pudding must be to a proper Britisher. This chocolatey mouthful of holiday hedonism goes by the unlikely name of Grasshopper, probably because two layers of frosting are green. There is no possible way to consider these budget baking, unless you can restrain yourself to a batch or two and restrict the treat to Christmas. Since I found this in *Bon Appétit* magazine several years ago, I've seen several similar recipes which don't look quite so good. The difference, I think, may be the quantity of butter and the nuts. Be sure to use real butter, unsalted, and to toast the nuts lightly, as directed. These store beautifully—if you forget where you put 'em.

Grasshoppers (makes 40 bars)

1½ cups sifted flour
2 cups sugar
¾ cups plus 2 tablespoons instant cocoa
   (I like Swiss Miss for this)

1½ teaspoons salt
1 teaspoon baking powder

———

1⅓ cups butter
4 eggs
2 teaspoons vanilla
2 tablespoons corn syrup

———

2 cups coarsely chopped toasted nuts
(walnuts or pecans)

 * Mint Frosting
 ** Chocolate Glaze
*** Icing for Wreaths

Preheat oven to 350°F. Sift first five ingredients. Add butter, eggs, vanilla, corn syrup, mixing thoroughly. Fold in nuts. Spread batter in oiled 9 x 13 x 2 pan. Bake 40 to 45 minutes until soft in center and edges are slightly firm. Do not overbake. Cool.

* Mint Frosting

2 cups sifted powdered sugar
¼ cup (½ stick) softened butter
2 tablespoons milk
1 teaspoon mint extract
green food coloring

Combine and mix. Spread over cooled pastry. Place in freezer 15 to 20 minutes to harden. Cut pastry into 40 bars but do not remove from pan.

** Chocolate Glaze

2 squares unsweetened chocolate
2 tablespoons butter

Heat together and brush evenly on top of frosting. Allow to harden in refrigerator. Carefully re-cut and remove from pan.

*** Icing for Wreaths

2 to 2½ tablespoons milk
½ cup powdered sugar
green food color

Add enough milk to make firm. Mix until smooth. Stir in color. Pipe wreaths onto cookies.

Store tightly covered between waxed paper or freeze.

Saving a dollar here and there in Christmas baking does not put presents under the tree. Or in the stockings, in our family's case. Since our first Christmas together, my husband and I have filled stockings for each other. We never let it go with an almond in the toe, a bunch of oranges and apples as fillers. Each year our stockings have become more and more opulent, proliferating from a simple, needed scarf, a couple pieces of chocolate, and some pretty bows to the point where putting one together costs as much or more than the "real" gifts under the tree.

That's okay for Jack. It's the one time each year he splurges. His stocking for me is always a sight to behold. Indeed, he even made the stocking—a brown suede, lace-up boot with four-inch braid bordering the top edge. Each year he makes it more magnificent than the last. It's his annual burst of creativity; the beautiful trim and complicated bows, unfamiliar to his fumbling fingers, represent hours of frustrating struggle. The love those bows express mean more to me than any of the goodies. But such goodies! Swiss chocolates, molded and tiny and wrapped in foils of Christmas design, each one individually tied with the narrowest of red-velvet ribbons, to the laces of my boot. Triangle after triangle of white Toblerone—memories of the year we survived a four-month European backpacking trip on a diet of bread and cheese and chocolate. And then fillers of more lasting value such as a watch, hand-sculpted earrings, and, each year, some sort of Christmas ornament, truly fine, no piece of Hong Kong mass production. Last year it was an Italian papier-mâché angel robed in red. The year before it was two tree ornaments of sculpted stoneware—a soldier and an angel—from a museum shop downtown.

I try to do something similar for him. But this year I was ever conscious of the cash constraints. Snob that I am, the only suitable ornament I could find cost sixty dollars—way too much, especially for an ornament that wasn't totally perfect.

Lord, I know you must laugh at us each year, it being your birthday we celebrate—by buying gifts ostensibly for each other but really for ourselves. But can you help me anyway? I need a gift for Jack. I know he'll stuff his stocking for me with the outpouring of his heart. I see him sneaking surprises up to his bureau each night when he gets home from work. What do I have for him? A wallet and socks. Some gift! Should I make something? Nothing's inspired me, even if I could find any extra midnight hours in which to do it. And I know you don't want me to give him some sixty-dollar gimcrack!

Quick as a whistle it came, the idea for the gift and the poem to go with it.

Did he like the poem? Yes. I found it in his jewelry box (which I happened to open because JC saw it on his bureau and inquired as to the unfamiliar object's identity, it being rare that Jack has it out). He had it out to stow away the poem for safekeeping.

And the gift? When guests inquired, as they will, about the gifts under the tree, it was the first thing he showed. It is a wreath, maybe six inches in diameter, made from two stuffed and braided ropes of cranberry-red Christmas calico. In the center, dangling by a ribbon of red satin, is a heart—one side made of the red calico, the other side from a scrap of antique white satin. Trimming the heart and entwined through the wreath to form a small bow at the top, for hanging, was antique white lace he recognized immediately. It was left over from the roll of lace used on my wedding dress. And the poem? That's personal.

JC was another matter. **Sentimentality doesn't stretch far with a five-year-old.** We bought her a dollhouse. Had it been the year before, I would have gone for a luxury model, a dreamhouse of a dollhouse, one to pass from generation to generation. But what does she care about the next generation? And how could I predict if she would even *care* about a dollhouse? She certainly hadn't indicated an inclination. The dollhouse in the church bulletin seemed a reasonable risk, only thirty dollars. The construction certainly wouldn't win any prize, it was obvious immediately, but what spectacular design! Three stories, two porches, turrets, even an attic! I wondered about the wallpaper, but the garish patterns (obviously a child's choice!) she loved. A mother should know better. Why try to foresee the taste of a daughter who uses the dollhouse's Victorian toilet's water tank as a breadbox!?!

Her stocking we stuffed with furnishings for the dollhouse. We didn't buy a houseful, nor did we buy collector's quality. "It's *her* dollhouse, Cam," my husband told me. "She doesn't care if it's plastic." Now she's busy earning money so she can make improvements. With furniture? No. Miniature mice.

In making our Christmas buying plans for children we tend to forget that ours won't be the only gifts under the tree. Presents from grandparents and great-aunts are a sure thing. Reassured by their record of success, we made fewer of our own purchases. The items she'd need in the next few months were our Christmas gifts: a backpack, a new leotard and tutu, and a crayola carousel which seemed a bit superfluous since she had so many art supplies already. Now I don't know how we got along without it (she and her mother share at least one fault—we're never quiiite organized).

Still there was the problem of her traditional ornament. Every year we buy her one and mark in the Christmas logbook that it is hers. In that Christmas Future when she has her own tree, probably someplace far from us, we'll know she has a bit of Christmas Past. But—it finally dawned!—a few days make no difference for an ornament intended for her tree of 2010. Why not revise the tradition slightly? Why not buy that ornament (and any we might like for trees between now and that Christmas three decades away) on the twenty-*sixth* of December instead of the twenty-*fourth*? Half-price sales mean twice as many ornaments or ornaments twice as nice or money to be "saved." We combined the three. We also started Alexis's collection. How could I rationalize a couple more? Jack's birthday is two weeks after Christmas. His celebration gets lost in post-holiday humdrums. Clothes are his usual birthday gifts—logical, since January clearance sales present an opportunity to restock the closets. Slipped in with the shirts and trousers, Jack found two ornaments—one from each of his daughters. (I think we've stumbled onto a new tradition.)

Christmas ornaments make great gifts. There's never a wrong size or bad match and they need not be expensive. They're welcome relief to the teacher who's still lathering up and scenting her underwear with the twelve-year supply of scented soap she gets each year. One's tree, on the other hand, always appreciates an addition. I love to remember the whys and wherebys of each bauble as I hang it year after year after year. Each one brings to mind people and places I might otherwise forget. Where we live, the shops and craft shows are loaded, from Labor Day on, with one-of-a-kind decorations regularly priced from three dollars up—this in a town where florists ring up seventy-five cents each time they sell a single pine cone in December! Ornaments are bargains. Ask for a discount if you're considering several.

If you have time, you can make your own. Some of course require more talent and tools than others, but the most charmingly decorated trees I've ever seen reveal more cleverness than cash resources. We have beloved ornaments which identify our Christmas tree as ours. Not using them would be unthinkable. But if something ever happens to them, I know I can still come up with a stunning tree—to an objective eye, perhaps prettier than the one we have—for under fifteen dollars. How? With scads of ribbon and a little help from nature.

The ribbon would be deep and rich, either red or green, satin or velvet, tied into bows with *long* tails. Whether fat and fun or skinny and sophisticated, I'm undecided. I *do* know that to buy enough rich ribbon to robe the tree right I'd have to watch for sales and get quantity discounts, not difficult in most shops in summer. I might go "country" and make my own ribbon out of Christmasy calico. Either way, the tree would be covered in ribbon.

Its only other (or substitute) adornment would be dozens of ornaments made of ribbon and Queen Anne's lace, made by pressing lots of those delicate-looking weeds either on a flower press or in a telephone book.

> Remove the stems, place about four blooms per page, allow one-half inch of pages between flowers to serve as cushion, weight down the book, and put it in a dry, warm place. After about a week of drying in the book, cover the flowers with a spray glue (and—optional—sprinkle glitter on both sides). Tie a ribbon loop with a bow on top; glue the bottom of the loop to the back of the flower. It's ready to hang.

A simple, stunning beauty is a tree hung with several dozen of these. But better to have none than not enough, especially if that's all your tree is wearing. I found the instructions for the Queen Anne's lace ornaments, along with eighteen others, in *Sunny O'Neil's Favorite Christmas Decorations* (Sunny O'Neil, 7106 River Road, Bethesda, Maryland 20817—$2.00). The author has decorated several trees for the Smithsonian Institution and contributed to White House decorations. Unlike many of the holiday ideas in craft books and magazines, hers are not cute or gimmicky. Write for her booklet if you admire lovely, old-fashioned decorations such as the Queen Anne's lace ornament or tabletop trees of ribbons or cones and pods. Among the instructions in her booklet are some for dried flower wreaths, the kind florists and craft shops tag for at least twenty to thirty dollars. Guess what I'm giving for Christmas next year?!

10

Living on the Fringes?

Dishonest money
dwindles away,
but he who gathers
money little by little
makes it grow.

PROVERBS 13:11

When the job goes, so do the fringes. You won't miss the free parking space, but what about health and life insurance? Disability? A pension or retirement fund? The temptation is to gamble the long shot, to let these expenses slide. But what happens if you lose, if an emergency catches you short?

The financial cloud hanging over a job's termination is one of those which can be said to have a silver lining. Employers who provide insurance usually also provide pension funds, annual leave, and, if you leave involuntarily, severance pay. Your exit may mean a windfall of extra cash, and through shrewd planning you may offset your losses with your gains.

Take my own situation. Alas, no free car or poolside condo came with the job, but I did benefit from free health and life insurance. Also, both the company's retirement and deferred profit-sharing accounts held funds intended for my "sunset" years. By quitting at age thirty, I lost all my retirement and much of my share of deferred profits, as well as both insurances. Having worked for that employer for only four years, I received only 40 percent of my share of deferred profits, each year of my employment pro rated for 10 percent. But the check representing that 40 percent was welcome, as was the check for unused vacation time. Because my exit was voluntary, there was no severance pay.

Health insurance we didn't replace, as my company plan didn't cover the family, only me. All of us are under a family policy my husband has through his own employer. His is not free, as mine was. In fact, we pay top dollar for it, but it's the best available and a necessity in a household with two young children. Neither did I replace my life insurance. My husband is well-covered through his employer, and I am covered by both a small whole-life policy (taken out by my father for me several years ago when he could get a discount on what was already a bargain-basement rate) and a term policy through my college alumnae association. I like to think I traded "some-day, maybe" compensation (medical expenses, retirement income, life insurance) for cold cash now.

No one's situation will duplicate mine, but when you sit down to appraise the potential budget mandated by your reduced circumstances, it's important to tabulate new expenses as well as the few one-time-only financial resources. First, what may constitute your own windfall?

INCOME YOU WON'T GET IF YOU KEEP YOUR JOB: A ONE-TIME WINDFALL

Severance Pay. Who receives it and how the amount is calculated vary. The only sure thing is: quitters don't get any. But if you leave a job involuntarily after several years with that employer, there should be some compensation. It may be as little as a week's pay or as much as a month's. If you aren't approached by a personnel officer, assume the initiative. *Before* you leave the job, get it in writing (whatever "it" is in your case). This money is taxable income and may not come in a lump sum.

Unused Leave. Employers owe you unused accumulated vacation time whether or not you leave by choice. You should receive a lump-sum check before or soon after you leave, or it may be included in your final paycheck. You'll owe the regular taxes and social security on it.

Retirement Plan Refunds. Pension or retirement

plans and the rules governing them vary from employer to employer. If only your employer contributed to your account and/or you're under a stipulated age and/or you worked in that company for just a few years, you probably won't get much of a refund, if any. But if you contributed from your earnings, you're owed at least that much. Dig out your contract! Plan on paying taxes next April *if* the refund was employer-contributed *and* you don't "roll it over" into a retirement fund you establish (probably an IRA) immediately (within 60 days). If the money was your own (you contributed it), it has already been taxed. You can use it to meet current needs or you can invest it. But if the employer made the contribution it has probably not been taxed, the idea being that it would stay idle until you're in the low-income, sunset years for which these funds were established, when it would become taxable but at a lower rate. Note: contributions made in 1973 or earlier qualify for long-term capital gains; only 40 percent is taxed. If the amount is sizable (more than a few hundred dollars) talk to your personnel officer or, better yet, a financial consultant; you don't want any extra, unexpected headaches next April 15, by which date the law may have been changed again, knowing Congress!

Deferred Profit Sharing. Like more standard retirement-plan refunds, these vary company to company and must be rolled over into another tax-deferred plan, such as an IRA, if you want to escape immediate tax consequences. Your refund may not equal the amount deferred for you if your company's plan has a vesting clause which requires you work a certain number of years to collect 100 percent of what is put away for you. But IF you worked under the plan for several years, AND IF the plan's trustees invested the money wisely, you MAY receive a surprisingly large check. Mine, for instance, was 40 percent of its potential.

Unemployment Compensation. Sorry, you can't collect this if you quit. But if you're let go, you may be eligible for up to six months worth of benefit checks (which can be spread out over a longer period). Some people think there's a stigma attached to this income; remember that some of this money might have been yours—in your paycheck—if your employer had not made contributions to this fund on your behalf and for just such contingencies. The amount varies by locality and according to your most recent wage or salary. Also, you must, at every visit to pick up your check, prove you're looking for work. If you accept temporary jobs, your checks end temporarily but resume when the job ends. As soon as possible after your job ends, take your social security card and your official termination notice from your employer to the nearest unemployment office. Plan on waiting a few weeks before the first check arrives. Depending on what your W-2 (total yearly income) shows, come tax time, you may owe taxes on part of what you collect.

WHAT TO DO WITH YOUR WINDFALL

Unemployment compensation will quickly dribble away on day-to-day expenses. Compensation for unused annual leave provides a nest egg for emergencies, as does severance pay. Lump-sum pension funds and/or profit shares are tricky. As explained earlier, you may need to roll them over into another tax-deferred vehicle if the tax consequences will be too heavy. But that makes them inaccessible as living expenses or as an emergency fund. When you withdraw from an IRA, you incur a

10 percent penalty, and you lose the tax-deferred status. Whether you roll the funds over depends on your tax bracket, the size of the lump sum, and the desperation of your financial circumstances. It's not likely you need all the money immediately, so make it work, or grow, for you until you do.

I didn't. I foolishly squandered mine on day-to-day expenses while it sat in a checking account. Passbook savings would have been nearly as foolish. Had I the opportunity to relive the situation, here's what I would do:

First, I'd design a twelve-month "balance sheet." I'd draw up a list of expenses, not detailed but showing due dates for all insurance premiums, taxes, holidays, and other anticipated, sizable expenses. Then I'd mark down all expected income, estimating how much would remain, after paying day-to-day expenses, to put toward those occasional big ones. Comparing the "probable outgo" to "probable income" would tell me *how much* of my windfall I'd need *when*. (That I would need to use the windfall during the next year or two is a foregone conclusion.) Then comes the fun part: scouting out high-interest savings vehicles with maturity dates that correspond to my anticipated due dates, the object being to make each dollar grow as much as possible until the day I cannot possible get along without it.

The trick is not merely finding the most dazzling interest rate. If only it were that simple! It's knowing my "new" tax bracket and figuring out the after-tax interest implications, espcially difficult in a year of personal financial flux. It's balancing favorable interest rates with liquidity and with safety (better, after all, to keep my windfall small but safe in a passbook savings account than lose it all in a risky, high-yield venture which founders). It's keeping my windfall liquid enough so I have the use of it even though it's not actually in my hands.

I'd make small investments in money markets or other certificates of deposit (CDs) with sixty, ninety-day, or six-month maturities. Because they mature so quickly, bankers consider CDs liquid assets and, therefore, acceptable security (collateral) for loans—actually loans from yourself to yourself. By law the lender (not you, but the banker) must charge interest at a rate at least one percentage point (more often, 4, 5, or 6) above that which your CD earns (to make sure you repay), but when it's time to square things with Uncle Sam you see that, after taxes, the rate on the loan was actually lower than (or comparable to) what you're simultaneously earning! That's because the interest you pay is tax deductible while interest you earn is tax free (up to an ever-decreasing maximum). The higher your tax bracket, the sweeter the deal. (Welcome to the world where you can spend your money and have it too! Did you ever imagine that you'd have to halve your income to get a crack at playing such financial high jinks?) By the way, this is not to suggest that you borrow (on the theory that tomorrow's money will be cheaper than today's). That's compiling debt—bad news. This is different—actually borrowing against yourself—quite different. You're still in the black.

A couple of things about the game of "high finance": the rules are ever-changing and they don't apply to everybody. For example, Congress established the All-Savers certificates as a one-year-only opportunity (1982) for a married couple who file jointly to earn up to two thousand dollars worth of tax-exempt interest. Otherwise, the interest ceiling for a similar couple was four hundred dollars and scheduled to be halved the following year! For players whose windfall is in the five figures, some form of Keogh Plan or IRA (Individual Retirement Account) is a partial solution—beyond the scope of this book. If you're considering an IRA or Keogh, perhaps attracted by their tax deferments, remember that most lenders don't consider either one a liquid asset. If you need to borrow from your plan and find an agreeable lender, the portion you use as collateral immediately loses its tax-deferred status. Also, the interest penalty is terrible.

There's one advantage in not rolling over lump-sum pension funds. If you meet certain qualifications, you can use ten-year averaging to soften the tax bite. You pay tax on the entire amount in one year, but the averaging method keeps you in a lower tax bracket. You figure the tax as if it were paid over a ten-year period *and* without reference to other taxable income that is yours in the year you collect the lump sum. The qualifications? You must receive all the money in a single tax year; you must have been a member of the pension or profit-sharing (or stock bonus) plan for at least five years *before* the year you collect; you must average *all* the taxable portion of the lump sum; you must be getting the lump sum because you retired or changed jobs (or left the one you're in). Also, if the plan was terminated *and* you're at least 59½ *and* you meet the other qualifications, you can use the averaging method. Obtain Form 4972 from the IRS. If you need to keep the lump sum readily available and suffer the tax consequences because you don't qualify for ten-year averaging, consider regular five-year income averaging, Form 1040, Schedule G from the IRS.

My "should have" plan did not use any windfall to replace lost benefits. I wouldn't have needed to, as explained earlier, except for disability coverage. I did not invest in disability (perhaps an unwise move) because I am not the sole source of income in our family. Disability coverage for at least one wage earner per household is mandatory. So are the following coverages, for which every household budget should make ample provision—perhaps applying some of the windfall.

LOST BENEFITS YOU'D BETTER FIND ROOM FOR IN YOUR BUDGET

Health Insurance. Should you not have a spouse with a policy that already covers you—or can cover you—it's vital that you take immediate precautions. Most policies terminate with the job or no more than thirty days later. New policies usually aren't valid for the first ninety days. Sometimes you can pick up, through your soon-to-be-former employer's insurer, a one-time temporary policy. Individual policies are increasingly rare and prohibitively expensive. You may be able to get a lower-cost group policy through a professional or alumni association. That reason alone may be worth the organization's membership fee. But if insurance is your reason for joining, check the policy first. Many give low coverage and require high deductibles. If you have a college degree and/or perceive yourself to be a professional, consider the Blue Cross/Blue Shield group-rate policy offered to members of the Association of Part-Time Professionals, whose membership fee is thirty dollars (see page 190).

Reams have been written on selecting health insurance. Policies vary according to region, your age and health, and company. None are cheap. An HMO (health maintenance organization), basically a prepaid health plan, is worth considering if there's a good one in your area. Otherwise, whatever you do, keep some kind of major medical for high-cost illness; the lifetime maximum should be at least $250,000, and there should be an annual limit, typically a $1,000 "stop-loss" on your share of costs. Two clues to a good policy are these contract clauses: recurrent disability (a relapse, if the illness occurs within six months of your first case, will not be treated as a new disability which would require a wait) and waiver-of-premium (if you become disabled, you can temporarily stop making premium payments). A high deductible—*if you conscientiously keep a few hundred tucked away,* perhaps in a money market or CD—may save you several hundred dollars annually on premiums.

Life Insurance. Like health insurance, life insurance has provided fodder for many an article, some good, some no help at all. There's always an audience because people crave assurance that their dependents' needs will be met. But if you have no dependents, forget life insurance, at least for the financially strapped time being. If you have dependents, here's a brief summary of what you should know.

There are two basic types of life insurance, each marketed in several versions. Whole-life types *typically* offer these three selling points: the premium stays the same no matter how old you get; if you don't die by a stipulated age you collect the insurance—or much of it; the premiums (and possible dividends) build up cash value you can borrow against. The primary disadvantage of whole-life is its cost. Especially now, when you need the most coverage for the least money, term insurance is a better buy, although your premium will increase as you grow older (probably every five years) and you become a greater risk. Few term policies reward you with a fat refund for reaching a grand old age; your policy may not, in fact, be renewable after you reach a certain age, usually sixty or sixty-five. Few term policies build up cash values you can borrow against.

> Don't let burial expenses drain the resources you leave for your loved ones. Insurance dollars and other assets can be better spent. You can spare your loved ones the snares and excessive expense (sometimes several thousand dollars) by arranging contingency funeral and burial plans now, while you're sound of body and mind. Such provision need be no more morbid than purchasing life insurance. A ten to twenty dollar investment in lifetime membership in a memorial society can save hundreds—or even thousands—of dollars that your family could better use for living expenses. See page 77 for details.

Companies set rates by age and, sometimes (especially for individual policies), by health as reported by your doctor. Look for a term policy that's renewable, that allows you to renew every five to ten years without a physical. Also look for a disability or a waiver-of-premium clause (the premium is automatically paid if you become disabled).

Group rates are usually better deals than individuals can get, but this is not always true. Alumni associations, professional organizations, church groups sometimes offer group policies. Compare several. If you're married, both spouses should be covered, even though one may not be employed at present. Don't waste money covering the kids. Insurance is for covering lost income; few children contribute to the family purse.

You need enough coverage to pay off outstanding debts (don't forget the mortgage insurance you may already have through your lender) and burial expenses. A nest egg for your heirs is nice, but remember social security credits you've accumulated and your spouse's ability to generate income.

> **There's More than One Access to Insurance Money!** Even though this is not the time to take out a whole-life policy, it may be the time to make use of one you already have. Use the cash value, an "extra fund" you wouldn't collect anyway if the policy matures (and your heirs couldn't collect it either).
>
> My policy is a small one ($5,000) my father gave to me when I turned eighteen, the last chance for him to purchase it at the reduced rates available for a minister's minor. The annual premium is sixty dollars. (Sorry, that low rate is virtually extinct. But the hundred dollars-plus it would cost today will seem similarly low in another decade or so: a sales pitch for whole-life but *not* adequate reason to be tempted. What's $5,000 today? That hundred dollars could buy term coverage worth several times that $5,000.)
>
> It had been my practice to use the policy dividend and the interest earned on the cash value to reduce my premium payment to about forty-eight dollars. The policy was still worth five thousand, but I wasn't giving the company use of my accumulated interest to invest at what amounted to a 5 percent return.
>
> But this year we needed more than that twelve dollar difference. The solution: I borrowed on my policy's cash value, which in the thirteen years of its existence had grown to between four and five hundred dollars. We used the money to help pay property taxes. The loan costs us 6 percent interest compounded annually. Being tardy with our taxes would have meant a 10 percent penalty as well as 14 percent interest.

Should I die before we repay the loan, the $5,000 insurance will be reduced by the part of the loan outstanding. But if I had died without borrowing that loan, my family would never get to use that cash value. They'd still get the flat $5,000.

Obviously, borrowing from a life insurance policy is not something you do for funds for a joy ride. But if you have the policy and need the money, don't forget that it's a good way to have your money and use it too.

Disability Insurance. Sometimes called "sickness and accident" insurance, your chances of collecting on this before you're sixty-five are several times greater than the chances of your heirs collecting on your life insurance. A recent *Changing Times* magazine article states, "At 35, the chances of suffering a serious disability before reaching 65 are one in three." The National Insurance Consumer Organization puts it bluntly: "If you're disabled you're still a financial burden to your family, but if you're dead, you're not."

One warning: disability insurance may be hard to obtain when you're unemployed. Too many people abuse the system by claiming disability when they're unemployed but capable of working, so insurers are wary. Neither do insurers like candidates who work in their own homes. However, insurers screen candidates carefully; your honest reputation should help.

The best policies, but the most expensive, are "non-cancellable with sickness" (also called "guaranteed-renewable") to the age of 65 and offer accident benefits for life with only a thirty-day wait. Almost as good is an "optionally renewable" policy; the insurer, to be rid of you, must cancel everybody in your category (i.e., everybody over fifty). Group policies are riskier but less expensive than individual ones. Some plans only cover long-term disability.

Obviously, shopping for disability insurance is complicated. The recent *Changing Times* article mentioned above is a good place to begin your homework. Ask for the April 1982 article "Disability Insurance. Are You Covered If You Can't Work?" (Write: *Changing Times*, 1729 H St. NW, Washington, D.C. 20006.)

• • •

Replacing benefits you forfeit with your job eats huge chunks of the windfall, but no less voracious are auto insurance, homeowners or renters insurance, property taxes. How does your shrinking budget cope with these expensive appetites? While you assess the implications of your windfall and new expenses on your financial balance sheet, consider how you can save money by reexamining what you get for your dollars spent on the following items.

WORKING THE KINKS OUT OF BUDGET BENDERS

Auto Insurance. Few simpler ways to waste several hundred dollars annually exist than to overpay for car insurance. Yet many people do it, some spending more each year they'd get if they totaled their car! Chances are you'll collect from your collision coverage or your fire or theft only once every ten or so years; even then it's not likely to be because your car is totaled. *If you conscientiously maintain an emergency fund of several hundred dollars*, you can cover the risks of minor accidents yourself, either by lowering your collision coverage or by raising your deductible. You may be able to save as much as one-third to one-half of your premium by raising the deductibles on the two major categories of your policy—the comprehensive to $200 and the collision to $500; any loss over $100 is a tax deduction anyway. Another way to chip dollars is to avoid duplicating medical coverage your health insurance already contains. You want liability coverage—lots of it—as a hedge against potential court costs. Raising bodily injury liability from the low five figures to one well up in the sixes is a wise way to spend some of the dollars you save by skimping on other coverages.

Non-drinkers, non-smokers, car-poolers (who would otherwise drive every day), drivers who've passed driver-education courses, school-age drivers who make excellent grades—these drivers can take advantage of special discounts made available but not always publicized by many insurers. Anti-theft devices, automatic seat belts, driving fewer than 7,500 miles per year, having a college-age driver attend school 100 miles or more from home—all these may qualify you for further discounts. The trick is finding the right company. If you have a bad record—accidents or serious traffic violations—your choices are limited. Otherwise, careful shopping can save you at least enough for a tune-up, maybe as much as a year's worth of fuel! Some state insurance departments publish insurance guides which compare company rates and coverage (which vary state to state as well as in other ways). You may find the lowest rates among companies that don't use agents, whose commissions come out of your premium!

Homeowners or Renters Insurance. You can't skip this. We once tried. Four months in an apartment didn't justify the bother or expense of renters insurance, we thought. We were burglarized twice!

Our tax deduction was a help, but it did not equal the insurance payment we could have claimed.

Homeowners insurance tends to be more expensive. You should have coverage equal to at least 80 percent of what it would cost to replace your home. A smaller coverage may mean your compensation is disproportionately lower, even if you have to replace only part of your house.

To save money, don't make the common mistake of including land value in the property you insure. Subtract the value of your foundation, too. And don't mistake your assessed value for the property's true value. The tax assessor's estimate (usually based on market value) can be either higher or lower than an insurer's estimated replacement cost. Compare several policies, and, if a deductible clause is available, consider taking it as a way to save some of this "gambled" money. As with car insurance, be careful that a hefty portion of your premium is not putting the steak on some agent's table; not all agents are unreasonable, but don't let convenience decide for you.

Property Taxes. A few localities assess, for tax purposes, your property's value by what you paid for it. Blessed are those homeowners who live in such a community and bought their homes long ago! Most places rely on guesstimates based on age, apparent condition, neighborhood desirability, features and improvements (number of baths and fireplaces, etc.) on record at city hall. If your locality uses the latter method, you may be able to have the guesstimate revised and your property tax lowered.

We did. We very politely voiced our disagreement by, first, telephoning the appropriate local office and, second, completing (by its due date!) the form they sent to us. We showed that the house interior was not yet in as fine a condition as the outside and the papers on record indicated. Also, the assessor had equated the number of chimneys (three) with the number of working fireplaces (one), an obviously wrong assumption but something we discovered only when we traipsed to city hall to peruse the file on our property. One tip: if the assessor asks to take a look inside your house, don't undermine your own efforts for lower taxes by presenting the place at its sparkling, unnatural best!

Mortgage Money. Lowering your mortgage payment is nigh unto impossible without selling your property. One thing you *can* do, though, is make sure you're not paying the lender unnecessarily for mortgage insurance, sometimes required by lenders until you've whittled the outstanding loan to where it's in "proper" ratio to the value of the property. Query your lender. Because federal regulations don't require you to be notified, they probably won't tell you unless you ask.

Should you have a low interest rate on your mortgage, you may be approached with an offer to refinance. Don't let the easy money tempt you; the deal's not likely to be as good as it appears. To evaluate this kind of offer, you must consider how much you'd lose by boosting the interest rate on your outstanding balance and add that into the cost of the funds you'd get by refinancing. Before you bite the bait, talk to a financially savvy banker who will consider the issue objectively. Another possibility is to order a reprint from *Changing Times*, "That Offer to Refinance Your Mortgage—Good Deal or Bad?" July 1981. (Address is on page 180.)

Not to push *Changing Times* (I admit, as an ex-employee, an apparent bias), but a subscription to that magazine will pay for itself a dozen times over in a matter of months. The information that is the stuff of this chapter and a few others constantly changes, and while no publication can stay on top of all of it, *Changing Times* does the best job. I know. As employees, we were expected to keep up with everything available in order to stay ahead of the competition. Despite my absence, the magazine still does!

11

Compromising
Situations

*All hard work brings
   a profit,
 but mere talk leads only
   to poverty.*

PROVERBS 14:23

A recent book title says it all—*The Joyless Economy*. Not that a job should be one oversized playground for grown-ups, but it should stimulate, offer variety, and provide opportunity for self-esteem, personal growth, and self-expression. Many jobs don't. If the job is not the problem, the schedule is. Frustrated workers console themselves with the security of paychecks and the countdown toward retirement. Unemployment appears the only option. But it's not. One out of six Americans has already discovered the part-time alternative.

Mine was the ideal opportunity. The business of writing and editing requires little more than a typewriter, paper, a few erasers, and the two big ones—a market and some uninterrupted quiet. Occasionally the latter means working nine-to-five, the *other* nine-to-five while most of the rest of the population is in repose. But my schedule is my own. I work when I want, where I want, for whom I want. And my work is what I want to do. Contacts from my days as a full-timer provide a market. That's not to say opportunities come knocking at my door; as often as not, I have to bang on theirs. But there are doors, and if the products I offer fill needs, those doors open.

A rarely realized concept—fulfilling one's own needs while meeting the needs of others! It needn't be. Traditional lock-step roles, where assembly line production mandates hours and environment, are filled by fewer than 20 percent of today's workers. Work patterns imposed on the other 80 percent are unnecessary carry-overs from the days when "work" meant an eight-hour stint at the factory. Today's service and information technologies imply a potential for flexibility, for self-employment, for part-time employment, for meeting one's own needs while simultaneously meeting society's. Secretaries, sculptors, cab drivers, computer programmers, teachers, tax collectors, police officers, and piano tuners: any role, you name it, part-timers can play it, either through independent endeavor or within the system.

Sometimes the role for which we're best cast is the one we try to escape. Perhaps you'd like yours better on a **part-time/or stay-at-home** basis. Or if your employer can no longer afford you full-time, part-time or job-sharing may be solutions. You still gain free time and freedom from the inflexibility that accompanies a five-day, nine-to-five existence, yet you retain a somewhat steady income and your employer retains your contribution. Believe me, your whole perspective changes when you're not accountable for every moment of a forty-hour week.

A friend of mine, an office worker, had *had* it with her job. Pregnancy was her perfect alibi for exclaiming, in effect, "Good riddance!" She resigned. But within a few months she realized that not all of her job was as horrible as she had thought. She actually missed aspects of it. And her employer missed her valuable contribution. Five years as a steady, reliable employee was her recommendation when she asked for—and got—a part-time, at-home renewal of her job.

Another friend, a nurse, works a ten-hour shift or two each week at the hospital. She fills in for absentees and in emergencies. The hospital appreciates her availability, and she appreciates the income. Her hourly wage as a part-timer is slightly higher (unusual) than when she was on salary, and she considers the occasional night of lost sleep when they call her for the night shift a small price for her "extra" daytime hours.

Part-time isn't limited to nurses and clerical workers. The twenty-first century "electronic cottage" envisioned by Alvin Toffler has already arrived. A few farseeing corporations have discovered they save money on pricey uptown office space *and* keep valuable employees content by setting up word-processors and computer consoles in workers' homes, cottage-industry style. Other businesses are experimenting with job-sharing, hiring two part-timers instead of one full-time person to perform a set of tasks.

So how do you convince your boss the part-time concept is a great one whose time has come? Present a solid case of its merits:

Your rested mind and body should result in **increased productivity.** Managers realize low energy and low motivation go hand-in-hand with low productivity.

Your **absentee rate** will be **zero** or greatly reduced. Studies show part-timers take less time off work (both for coffee breaks and sick days) because they take care of personal needs on their own time.

Part-time work gives your boss the opportunity to **match your skills to the task** instead of the clock. Employers like flexibility in scheduling.

You're **not as likely to burn out** as fast as someone who wearily chugs away at the daily grind. Studies show part-timers have less turnover, remain faithful to the employer.

Show your boss how you could **better use your time—and company time**—through a reduced work week. Obtaining 70 percent of the results for 50 percent of the money is a difficult enticement for a boss to pass up.

Negotiating for a new job that you'd like to be part-time may be more difficult. The Association of Part-Time Professionals (see box) has honed these recommendations:

Know your marketable skills and what you want.

Show those skills on a proper résumé that does not include the fact that you want part-time work; otherwise, you may not get an interview in which to explain yourself and your motives.

Before that interview, **know everything you can about the job** you want. Can it be split, pared, shared?

Also **find out,** ahead of time, **if the company hires other part-timers** and the "deals" they've worked out.

Should the employer seem wishful but hesitant, **offer to work on a trial basis,** perhaps even for free, for a short time.

What do you forfeit by working only part-time? The excuse to slough-off during working hours (no late lunches or half-hour coffee breaks). The wages of a full-timer (as well as being paid for fewer hours, you may get less per hour). Job benefits such as health and life insurance, profit-sharing, and a retirement fund. Quick promotions—or any at all.

Part-time work can be tricky from both your standpoint and your employer's. Your working only part-time does not relieve your employer of paying social security taxes or contributing to unemployment on your behalf. The number of hours you're hired for may depend on these considerations. The schedule you devise can be highly irregular but must fit your employer's convenience. Commuting several times weekly seems the worst possible solution; better to work one or two full days than retain the bother and expense of a five-day-week commitment.

The good news is the fact that the number of part-time jobs available is on the increase; the bad news is that the increase is partially due to the ailing economy. Many companies can't afford to continue at the same pace. Your prospects are exceptional if you have skills in accounting, data processing, engineering, health care, bookkeeping or other clerical work (especially if you speak a second language or use computers), or support services (such as home maintenance, day care for children).

One out of six Americans works part-time regularly and by choice. Two million of these are professionals, managers, administrators. How many people would like to join the ranks of the part-timers' army? Quite a few, thinks the Association of Part-Time Professionals. This non-profit, national organization exists to build acceptance of part-time as a management tool for employers as well as a work option for employees, particularly professionals, managers, and administrators. Criterion for membership is loose—"any job requiring a college degree or the work equivalency." That includes, but is not limited to, retired professionals, parents with family responsibilities, women reentering the work force, mildly disabled individuals, and gradaute students. For their thirty dollars membership fee, members get empathy and practical support. APTP issues a quarterly newsletter and informational brochures, operates as a resource center and "advocate," and provides group-rate prices for life insurance, health insurance, and similar employee benefits frequently unavailable to the part-timer. Local chapters (there are only six so far, but you can help start one) offer job referrals, monthly newsletters, and workshops. (Write: APTP, P.O. Box 3419, Alexandria, Virginia 22302.)

At least two successful part-timers have recently published books to aid others who want out. The books tend to duplicate each other in factual offerings, but each is worth a trip to the library or a perusal at your bookstore. The best I've found—but expensive ($15.95)—is *Look for a Part-Time Career for a Full-Time You* by JoAnne Alter, published by Houghton Mifflin (1982). Alter's part-time experience runs from sales clerk to camp counselor to typist to teacher. She covers dozens of possibilities and gives advice for accomplishing them. Another new book is *555 Ways to Earn Money* by Jay Conrad Levinson, who a few years ago wrote *Earning Money Without a Job*. Levinson's new book, published by Holt, Rinehart & Winston (1982), sells for $9.95 and aptly fits his personal philosophy of "patchwork economics."

PAID-FOR PLAY

Sometimes the elixir for job malaise is not less of the same (i.e., fewer hours at your old task). Maybe you can pick up those few crucial dollars through at-home self-employment that's an extension of what you dream of doing with your new free time, another way of filling your own need while meeting society's. How to discover an appropriate need? Brainstorm. Pick the brains of your family, friends, acquaintances. What do they think you do well? Tie the results together with the skills you know you have (or can easily acquire) and the needs you spot in your community or in your fields of interest.

Start by scanning this list of money-makers. I know they're money-makers because I know of people who have ventured successfully into each one listed; all of them are "need-fillers," therefore, lucrative. Just don't expect to get-rich-quick! Not every one is right for every person, of course—or for every community. Most might be said to be "woman's work," but after all, I am a woman and these are all options I considered for myself. Adapt them as you're inspired. Share them with your friends.

Small-time Catering Business. It needn't be gourmet or of wedding reception proportions. Two young women in our community capitalize on the busy schedules common to most local households. They offer "pick-up or deliver" casserole dinners to customers who don't have time to shop or cook for houseguests—or for themselves. Because the menu is limited—four types of casseroles sized according to need—the caterers need not keep a wide variety of spoilable food on hand. Their idea could be broadened by adding salad, bread or rolls, and dessert. Some people even lack time to run to the bakery, so merely assembling commercially prepared baked goods is a service and means extra profit. All you need to begin is a few extra casserole dishes (customers return emptied ones) and some simple but delicious recipes. Don't price yourself out of a market, but remember that your potential customers' alternative may be a hefty resturante bill.

Birthday Cakes, Gifts, or "Treat of the Month" for the Away-From-Home. You need a nearby campus or nursing home or hospital to make this successful, and you need access to your customers—the folks back home who pay the bill. Easiest access may be through the potential recipients! Sometimes an understanding staff person can help if you present your case appealingly. Two young fellows, students at a nearby university, put themselves so handily through school this way that they stayed in business after graduation.

Cake Decorating. Many bakeries can use an extra hand, especially at holiday times. So can busy homemakers or motherless homes where a cake is *de rigueur* for family celebrations but kitchen hands are all thumbs at decorating. Your customers can deliver their baked cakes which you decorate. Advertise with some sensational donations to a "high-visibility" event, especially one where refreshments wouldn't ordinarily be found. Beside your cake place a sign and several cleverly designed business cards which suggest holidays that regular baker/decorators might miss: April Fools', May Day, Mother's Day, Fourth of July, wedding anniversaries, etc. When you approach a bakery, take a sample or two of your work.

Candy. Bakeries and specialty shops of all descriptions cater to the whims of customers in search of old-fashioned flavor or style. They may be eager buyers if you have an attractive, tasty product or one that isn't otherwise locally available. I know of a woman in the hinterlands of Virginia (her town's population numbers only a few hundred) who buys chocolate molds from New York City (where she's never been) by catalog. She provides shops and party givers with the crazy designs people frequently want to use but seldom do because they're unavailable. She makes a tidy income by making them available.

Potential for lucre from your kitchen varies, of course, according to your ability. But why not whip up a little profit if you can? A brand-new book to check is *Cashing In on Cooking* by Nancy Baker. If you can't find it locally, the publisher is Contemporary Books, 180 North Michigan Avenue, Chicago, Illinois 60601. Cost is $8.95. A slightly older book (1979) is *How to Turn a Passion for Food into Profit* by Elayne J. Kleeman and Jeanne A. Voltz, published by Rawson, Wade.

Cooking Classes. If yours is the first dish emptied at the picnic or potluck, you should have no problem finding students. Just let the word slip that you're offering classes. If they're for adults, you may need to pick a theme: ethnic, thirty-minute gourmet, low-sodium, baking, etc. If you live in a neighborhood of working mothers or single fathers, offer classes for kids whose moms or dads don't have time or talent to teach them but would pay for this sort of educational child-care. Two women near me "borrow" a church kitchen where they teach (for fifty dollars per student) nine-to-thirteen-year-olds what to do with a whisk and a frypan. They cover the techniques of baking, broiling, roasting, preparing salads—everything anyone needs to know to prepare a meal.

Finishing Classes. The same parents who are too busy to teach their children to cook are often too tired by dinnertime to teach table manners. Also, it's an unusual child who does not respond more positively to a teacher and dinner table that's not the every day one. Large department stores run whole courses on the white-glove way of life. Why not offer a "fun" etiquette course in your home? You could charge three to five dollars per lesson, depending on your costs, for each of four to ten children of similar age. A dozen lessons at three dollars each is small price for a parent to pay for a well-mannered child!

Repair Sitter. Matching their schedules to those of repairmen is a problem for folks who work full-time. You can be there to greet the person who'll fix the dishwasher "between ten and four." You save the homeowner an extra trip home and several hours of lost pay; meantime, you catch up on postponed reading and collect a small fee.

Jack-and-Jill Skills. Choose a job you never had

time for when working, and let it be known you're available to perform that service for others. It may be something as banal as painting the back fence or laundering curtains. If you're cheerful, neat, and efficient, you'll have a waiting list in no time.

Gift Wrapping. Some people have neither the time nor the talent for this always-needed-at-one-time-or-another job. Busy nearby stores may need an extra, at-home hand, too. You can develop a coupon system or let the store make pick-ups and deliveries. You need huge rolls of only two or three all-purpose wrapping papers; coordinate the ribbon or trim to the paper to suit the occasion.

Bed and Breakfast. Make a spare bedroom available to occasional strangers. You needn't provide a separate bath—just a clean one. You can use free advertising mediums, such as nearby universities, local professional associations, and businesses that might refer clients or guests of employees. A well-worded press release (make it short but so it reads like a story) sent to metropolitan newspapers nationwide (address it to their travel section) may bring in all the business you can handle. Or you can put out a small amount of cash and join a referral service or list your home in various B & B directories. Betty Rundback, with the help of her daughter, turned a little kitchen-table operation—a directory of a few dozen names—into a fat book which gives readers access to 2,000 homes. It took her less than five years, that's how B & B is booming! This mother/daughter team has just published a "how to" pamphlet for those interested in starting a B & B. You can get it for $2, but be sure to specify what you want. (Write: Betty Rundback, RD2, Box 355A, Greentown, Pennsylvania 18426.) See page 147 for more on B & Bs.

Tour Guide. Living in a convention-oriented community is convenient, of course, but living in an area slightly off the commercially beaten track means less competition. Every business has occasional guests. Even the mom-and-pop operations—where the moms and pops are so busy with their hardware store or drycleaner or whatever that they have not a spare minute to entertain guests. You can be the family "friend" who guides visitors through the local landmarks, whether they be historic or merely entertaining. Bakeries, for instance, can be fun. So can factories or farms—any experience which the guest would not have otherwise.

Teacher/Tutor. Piano and ballet are usually the first claimed. But what about the oboe? Irish jig? Don't underestimate people's curiosity. Don't forget adults as potential students. And don't underestimate your own skills.

Crafts. Just because it's homemade doesn't mean it's desirable. Cutesy kitsch usually receives the little attention it deserves. (Some people try to sell the kind of artifact my kindergartner brings home!) But "country" is big business these days, especially in the chic city stores. You don't have to be able to blow beautiful glass baubles to bring home more than pin money. Someone who peddled their wares to a shop near us must be laughing all the way to the bank; odds and ends of wood scraps, as small as two inches square and as large as three inches by four, are sold for four to seven dollars each. The trick? Old-style colored "milk" paint and a few primitive brush strokes of black for windows and doors *et voilà!*—a village of charming homes and storefronts. A morning of mass production might produce an entire county! Another shop carries Raggedy Anns and Andys that move as quickly as the shopkeeper can get them from the dollmaker in Vermont. But these aren't the kind preprinted on a bolt of fabric. The shopkeeper sells—for twenty to twenty-six dollars each—the real thing, with button eyes and hand-stitched smiles. Her monkeys and kangaroos and donkeys, made from gray socks and by craftspeople in North Carolina, fetch between fifteen and twenty dollars. Other moneymakers: andirons, autoharps, canoes, cat dishes, weathervanes, wedding dresses, ox-yokes and yo-yos.

Finding a market, working out payment, and providing adequate supply can be big problems for the craftsperson with visions beyond the local church bazaar. Sometimes a craftsperson can be likened to a prophet: not without honor except in his own land! Don't be discouraged by lack of local success. Contact local shops and big stores first, of course, but consider swanky big-city markets. Remember, when approaching big stores, that each department has its own buyers. What one doesn't want another might. Take samples to antique dealers; sharp ones complement their inventory with new but obviously handmade merchandise. The folksy look of a doll on a rocker, a train on a bureau, or an herb wreath on a table spells charm. Sign up for crafts fairs—not just the little neighborhood type but the several dozen major ones you discover through other craftspeople and crafts publications. Some fairs offer an opportunity to meet city buyers, potentially steady customers. Crafts fairs also present an opportunity to keep 100 percent of the selling price. Otherwise you'll sell wholesale or by consignment. Wholesale price is usually 50 percent of what your product finally sells for, but that method is preferable to consignment (also about 50 percent) where your crafts may return shopworn and unsold. Selling crafts on a large scale demands careful planning. There's lots of competition. But the market is huge, as a multitude of publications indicate. A few dollars and hours on preliminary homework can save you time and money wasted on unmarketable goods.

The shopkeeper getting rich off Raggedies recommends *The Goodfellow Catalog of Wonderful Things, Number Three*, best described by its own subtitle, "a guide to America's finest crafts." "We *all* use it," she says, referring to herself and other buyers. But that doesn't mean they all buy the book; its price is $19.95. Find a craftsperson who will lend you one or will share the purchase price. Not all booksellers have it, but you can order it directly from Goodfellow Catalog Press, P.O. Box 4520, Berkeley, California 94704. Add $2.50 for postage. What do you get for all that money? You get 720 pages of glorious goodies made by nearly 700 very successful craftspeople selected from 2,500 applicants. Each person's products are described, priced, and illustrated with at least one photograph. The craftsperson's photograph is also included, as well as his or her statement of "philosophy of work." Most important, so that individual buyers and shop owners can order directly, the craftsperson's address is listed. The catalog is an unbeatable resource for learning what sells and for how much. It's also great advertisement if you're accepted for inclusion (and take heart—a few of the entries are novices).

Another resource widely recommended is *Creative Cash* by Barbara Brabec. This 208-page book, published by H. P. Books of Arizona, is available through bookstore chains such as Walden's and B. Dalton's and costs $7.95. If you live where supplies are scarce or expensive, you may be able to use another book (same price and by the same publisher), *Catalog Resources* by Margaret A. Boyd. It is just what its title says: it lists 2,000 places to find stuff you need.

An all-around value is *The National Directory of Shops/Galleries, Shows/Fairs* which incorporates and expands the former *Craftworker's Market*. More than 600 pages give regional markets, business aspects (bookkeeping, copyrights, marketing techniques, etc.), and tips by craftspeople and buyers. It sells for $12.95 and is widely distributed. Or write to Writer's Digest Books, 9933 Alliance Road, Cincinnati, Ohio 45242. Annual editions are published each March.

For a continuous free supply of inspiration and potential markets, get yourself on the mailing list of several "tony" mail-order catalogs—Horchow's, Geary's of Beverly Hills, Country Loft, Charles Keath Ltd.

● ● ●

Whatever your choice of money-making avocation, you need to spread the word that you're in business. You can't fill a need unless people let you! Word-of-mouth has a justified reputation as the best form of advertisement—not just because it's free. But how to start those mouths?

Show samples. Make yourself visible, known. Produce quality. A prominently patterned, well-hung wall of paper in your foyer—not in an out-of-the-way bedroom—produces comments and customers if wallpapering's your interest. It's the same principle as the sensationally decorated cakes. You'll be way ahead of some stranger from the Yellow Pages. Consider what catches your own eye. Meet that standard and exceed it—your best endorsement. The same standard holds for all advertising. Use free mediums. Church bulletins (not just your own), school and pre-school newsletters, inhouse business bulletins, bulletin boards at groceries and libraries and community centers; these are free vehicles for well-worded, well-designed notices that stand out from the usual hodgepodge. Pepper the market with business cards. Use colored ink or colored paper, an unusual letter style, and a pictorial design that suggests your business and the unique quality you lend to it.

People respond to creativity. And they use services and products that are *right there*, that don't have to be remembered or tracked down. You, by expending the energy of making yourself easily available, help insure the success of your venture.

The Last Word

A sign for a "lawn" sale enticed me into the tiny courtyard of one of a nearby neighborhood's $200,000-plus townhouses. Once inside, a fifty-cent mug caught my eye. The name of an upstate New York town I know well was worked prominently into the design. Aha! There's instant rapport among those of us who know from experience what it is to survive a Buffalo winter. Besides, the mug's owner and myself were of similar age and, as it turned out, left that area about the same time. But she had gone back there for nine months. Why? "Because," and she gestured toward the house she was apparently renting, "housing's so expensive in the Washington area!" Before she'd buy a house across the tracks, she'd move across the country. Or rent. Not that renting's wrong, but a thousand bucks a month is a lot to pay for two tiny bedrooms' worth of historic charm *anywhere*.

I heard an old-time camp meeting preacher belt it out this way last summer: "It's not making a living we worry about. It's maintaining a lifestyle!" He described that ex-Buffalonian well. Even Camilla squiggled in her seat just a little!

The imperative to distinguish "needs" from "wants" is an oldie-goldie, a rutted record too often trotted out, too seldom followed by its flip side: God wants to be there—through His people—to meet those needs genuinely beyond us. No wonder the flip side's less popular; it requires we look constantly toward God, in good times as well as bad, because we might (oh dread!) have to serve as agent!

Jesus always put it perfectly. It was easier for the stiff-limbed, stiff-necked camel to go down on its knees and wriggle, belly to the ground and neck doubled down, through the "needle"—the lowest gate in old Jerusalem—than for a rich person to enter the New Jerusalem.

As for humility? What do you say when you roll from your typewriter the last page of a book on how to survive a halved income and look up to find your life full of people living—in quiet contentment—on half of half?

Index